T0050676

A Technique for Meditation

A Technique for Meditation

Joseph Polansky

BOOKS

Winchester, UK
Washington, USA

First published by O-Books, 2011
O-Books is an imprint of John Hunt Publishing Ltd., Laurel House, Station Approach,
Alresford, Hants, SO24 9JH, UK
office1@o-books.net
www.o-books.com

For distributor details and how to order please visit the 'Ordering' section on our website.

Text copyright: Joseph Polansky 2010

ISBN: 978 1 84694 412 3

All rights reserved. Except for brief quotations in critical articles or reviews, no part of
this book may be reproduced in any manner without prior written permission from
the publishers.

The rights of Joseph Polansky as author have been asserted in accordance with the Copyright,
Designs and Patents Act 1988.

A CIP catalogue record for this book is available from the British Library.

Design: Lee Nash

Printed in the UK by CPI Antony Rowe
Printed in the USA by Offset Paperback Mfrs, Inc

We operate a distinctive and ethical publishing philosophy in all
areas of our business, from our global network of authors to
production and worldwide distribution.

CONTENTS

Introduction

There are so many meditative paths, techniques and procedures that the average beginner is overwhelmed and confused. There is a need for a simple, universal, methodology that will work for any one of any religious background.

The God we all worship is beyond name, form and system. The paths to Him are infinite. But without some form of regular, disciplined meditation, it is impossible to experience Him. Sincerity is the most important quality - sincerity and persistence.

This book originated as a home study course for the author's personal students. The lessons have been proven effective over the years. The course was designed so that if a person was stranded on a desert island with no books except this one, he or she would still be able to achieve the heart's desire and manifest all that is necessary.

Entire books can be written on each of the chapters here - the subjects are huge - but for the most part I tried to minimize the intellectual component and focus on the "practice". For, make no mistake, if the reader practices sincerely and faithfully, all the intellectual knowledge will come - easily, effortlessly and naturally. Doors in the mind will open and the knowledge will come flooding in.

Meditation is a "non-verbal" experience. This needs to be understood. If we are thinking "about" meditation or talking "about" meditation - we are not meditating. We are still in the intellect - the verbal level - the level of "maya" or "klipoth" as various traditions refer to it. This was another reason for minimizing the intellectual component. Our objective is to get the reader into the "actual" experience as quickly as possible.

As with all non-verbal experiences (sex, eating, drinking, breathing etc.) first comes the actual experience, only afterwards do we start to verbalize and intellectualize. This is the natural order of things. If we reverse the process - intellectualize before having the experience - we are in delusion. We will chatter, chatter and chatter, debate, argue and question and enter a verbal miasma from which it is difficult to extricate oneself.

One can read all the books about sex (and there are millions of them), one can discuss sex with all the experts and attain an ability to talk about sex very eloquently. But if one has not had the actual experience of sex one still doesn't understand it, in spite of all the intellectual knowledge acquired. It is only when one actually performs the sexual act that he or she can really understand all the books and verbal opinions. So it is with meditation. First have the experience and you will understand all the books. Have the experience and all the mortal questioning will cease. Arguments will cease. You have experienced something real and the verbal opinions and arguments are now meaningless.

This is the object of this book. We want the reader to have actual experiences in meditation - and to have them as quickly as possible and at the reader's own pace. Intellectual knowledge and explanations will come later - perhaps in other books. However it doesn't seem necessary. Any reader who practices what is written here will, in due course, be able to write their own books on the subject. No kidding!

Because relatively little is known about meditation here in the west, a whole mystique has arisen around it. Beginners naturally feel a sense of trepidation. But it is important for the reader (and I teach this to my students) to take the same approach to learning meditation as he or she would to learning how to play piano, or tennis, or any other art. In the beginning you can expect to make many mistakes, to have mixed results, and sometimes no results. Skill comes with practice. A student once asked the violinist Yasha Haifets "how do I get to Carnegie Hall?" And the master answered, "practice, practice, practice". So it is with meditation. It is a training - a skill - and it takes practice. Yes, beginners need some courses - a teacher - to start them off. But the real results come from practice.

The Master Musician leads a seemingly glamorous life. But the road to that glamor was definitely "unglamorous" - usually very mundane. Every day, sun shining or cloudy, he or she engaged in relatively unglamorous practice. Relentless practice - headache, toothache, love disappointments notwithstanding - there was relatively mundane, unglamorous practice. Practice of basics.

The meditative path, and the path to the Kingdom of Heaven, is similar. The practice is mundane, ordinary, and sometimes boring. Sometimes it is very hard work. It will lead us to places of great glamor and beauty, but the road to it is relatively unglamorous.

If the reader merely reads this as just another work of literature, very little will happen. But if the reader practices with each of the exercises given, the author can guarantee that he or she will have results. Over the years I have seen people try an exercise for a few days and report "nothing happened" - I couldn't do it - or some other such excuse. This is perfectly understandable. One must practice in a persistent and organized way. No one would expect to be proficient in anything worthwhile - golf, tennis, painting, art - you name it - in a few days. Yet, in meditation, there are many who have these kinds of unrealistic expectations. The reader/student needs to understand that immutable laws of the universe are being set into motion and that if one persists they **must** happen. The Sun would have to stop shining, the earth would have to stop its rotation, for these things not to work. The same forces are involved.

There are two subjects in this work that one doesn't find in the literature on meditation - yet these subjects are MOST important for success. The first is the need to "clear" the psychological debris that obstructs the meditation - and we deal with this in Part 2 and 3. If the reader is having problems getting results let him or her re-read these chapters and do the exercises. After doing the clearing work, then go back to your meditation. I could make the case that Part 2 and 3 are the most important sections of the book - especially for beginners. If these exercises are done properly all kinds of doors will open in the mind - and in very natural ways - almost imperceptible in the beginning - but over time will produce huge and positive changes.

There are many experienced meditators who say that all that is needed to "clear" obstructions is "awareness" - "presence". And this is certainly true. However when the clearing involves deep seated pain or powerful emotions most people (especially beginners) don't have enough "presence" or awareness to overcome these things. Thus they either need to find someone with "free attention" - with a strong sense of "Presence" - or do other kinds of exercises (such as in Part 2 and 3) to extricate themselves from their negative state. Little by little the attention and presence will get stronger and there will be less of a need for these exercises.

The other important subject that we deal with here is the need for "psychic self-defense". As one goes deeper into meditation one discovers that certain issues - blockages, obstructions, moods and feelings - are not really coming from one's own "baggage" but from outside oneself (outside the personal self). We live in an "ocean of thought and feeling" (as the meditator will discover as he or she proceeds). Thus many energies are impinging on us that are from "outside" ourselves (or so it seems) - that are coming from the environment and from people with whom we are in "psychic rapport". Thus the meditator needs to learn the skills of "protecting the aura" from outer infringement. There are various ways to do this, but in Part 12 and 13 we give workable ways. These too, will require practice until a momentum is built up. Also as one practices with parts 12 and 13 other ways to protect the aura will be revealed. In order to meditate effectively - to think our own thoughts and feel our own feelings - to enter into the consciousness that WE choose (and not some outer force) the aura must become like a "fortress" - inviolate. And this is the object of part 12 and 13.

This work is intended as a no-nonsense beginners guide to meditation. As much extraneous material as possible was left out - the focus is on the essentials. There is much more to meditation than is in this work. The author makes no pretense about this. But beginners need to start at the beginning and familiarize themselves with the basic tools that are available. As proficiency is gained in each of the exercises, new and more advanced information will come. This is the way things work.

As in any serious field, serious people, who practice and stay with it will get the best results. Dilettantes will suffer the same fate of dilettantes in any field - mixed or mediocre results.

I am of the opinion that Meditation is the Supreme Art and Science available to mankind. This is not to denigrate all the other wonderful arts and sciences. But a proficient meditator - by meditation alone - can acquire all knowledge in any field he or she chooses - thus it is the Mother of all the other arts and sciences.

Yes, it will require effort and practice on your part, but it is well worth it.

A suggested way to work with this book is to first read the whole thing in its entirety - just to get a general idea of what it is all about. Then take one chapter at a time and work with that exclusively for two weeks or even a month. Set aside time each day for this practice. After you have done all the exercises, start again from the beginning and repeat. Your new round will bring much deeper results than the previous one. You can continue the wheel of chapters as many times as you like. Each time will be new and different because your work will have a "cumulative" effect. Later on - after you've completed a few cycles - you can sort of pick up the book and see what exercise "calls to you" - and practice that. Each of the exercises are "infinite" in nature. Some people will have an affinity for sound and chanting meditations, some for color, some for affirmations.... this is in the natural order of things. You can take a chapter and make that your "specialty". (Some people will devote years to a certain kind of meditation, because that is their inner calling - but this is an individual matter.)

The Path

It is a wheel - like the wheel of a car
Spinning, spinning, spinning,
Endless repetition,
Spinning, Spinning, Spinning
The wheels don't feel like they are going anywhere
They just spin, spin, spin,
over and over
spin, spin, spin
But the driver, ah, He knows the destination
It is the spin, spin, spin that takes him to his goal.

The path is like a long walk through uncharted territory.
One step, then another, then another,
Step, step, step
Endless repetition
Through snow, ice, wind and rain
Step, Step, Step
Through hospitable and inhospitable places,
Step, Step, Step
The wayfarer should not tarry too long in any place,
Lest he lose his rhythm and momentum
Step, Step, Step
Progress seems slow, the path is endless,
But silent watchers have him under observation
At the right time, they pick him up and deposit him
at his destination.

Step, Step, Step.
The path itself is not glamorous
Though it leads to places of great glamor and joy.
Of itself, it is step, step, step.

Joseph Polansky

I

Thy Will Be Done

"Of all the mantras, incantations, and Words of Power, there is none as powerful as "Thy Will Be Done" uttered from a sincere heart."
The Magic Stone

The beauty of this type of meditation is that it is a "way of life more abundant"; of "fulfillment" rather than self-denial; of "self-expansion" rather the self-diminishment.

We make no pretense here of proclaiming "the one and only true way" of meditation. This would be absurd. There are many ways to meditate effectively - probably as many ways as there are people. This is merely ONE workable way.

This technique is designed so as not to conflict with anyone's religious beliefs. This is most definitely NOT our intention. But it is a way of penetrating to the sources of inspiration and revelation upon which most religions are based.

Don't be fooled by the simplicity of this meditation procedure. This author can testify that it takes LOTS of practice to attain to the simplicity and sincerity and inner integrity to perform it correctly.

Procedure

Sit in a comfortable chair (if you are ill or infirm you can practice this lying down in bed) and take a few deep; slow breaths.

Center yourself between the eyes. That is, put your attention between your eyes and stay there. Declare yourself to be an "Immortal Spiritual Being at one with God and in perfect union and harmony with the Universe."

(N.B. *** this is a Spiritual reality you know and this in itself is a nice meditation and well worth practicing for a few months or so.)

Envision a "bubble or aura of white light around you" and declare that only Light, Love, Truth, Wisdom, Good and Beauty may enter you and only these things may emanate from you. (This might take some practice to achieve, but if you persist you will achieve it.)

Say firmly - "My aura is sealed to all that is malicious and undesirable."

Envision a "White Brilliance" (like White Diamonds) above your head and start inhaling that brilliance into the body. See and feel it going into your lungs and from there into your bloodstream and from there into every organ and cell of the body. It is best if you can envision this, but if you can't rest in the knowledge that it is happening.

See this light purifying and cleaning every cell and organ. If this is done correctly, every cell and organ should be glowing with dazzling inner radiance. You can feel the light streaming from your fingers and feet. Your whole sphere (and if you want you can see your whole room) is permeated with this light.

If you feel that you "lack anything" - whether it be money or a "thing" or love or whatever. Envision it as being there in your auric sphere. Make a picture or speak the word for whatever it is.

Once you feel satisfied that you have "everything" you are ready to take the next and most important step. This is the ultimate and highest purpose of meditation. Put your attention above your head - about a foot above your head - and call on your own conception of God. Your own most High God. If its Jesus or Buddha or Jehovah doesn't really matter. Call on your God and ask that Its Will be done in your mind, body and affairs. That its light and power and love come into your mind and heart.

Don't try to "psychologize" God. Don't try to "push his buttons"; Don't try to negotiate or "make deals" with him; and don't attempt to dictate to him how He should run the universe.

If he is God Indeed He knows.

Rest in the power and light and vibration that will start to come through and just "let it" come through. "Let it happen".

You will feel when its time to "come down". When you do you should feel as if every question and problem is answered. You should feel a sense of peace and a "clarity". If you don't, go back and do some more "let thy will be done".

The correct attitude should be one of wanting Him on His terms and not on yours. If you do this, THAT will definitely and absolutely come in and the results (with time for the process is gradual) will be absolutely stupendous in terms of your well being on all your levels and dimensions.

If when you are in the stillness and silence of your communion (and the silence is really a dynamic silence - pulsing and powerful) and disturbing thoughts come to your mind you might try reciting a sentence of scripture (repeat it over and over); or chanting the five vowel sounds (AHH EHHH EEEE OOOO UUUU) over and over again; or chanting a sound like "OM" or "Amen". This tends to quiet the mind so that the experience of the "higher" can come in undisturbed.

Have a notebook on hand for when you come down from your meditation. Record there all your experiences, your feelings any pictures or messages that you might have seen or heard. Record there any people or faces that you see. Or visions or dreams. Everything is significant. And their meaning will unfold to you in due course.

You will be in a space of "revelation and inspiration" and you will be led to knowledges and powers and experiences too wonderful to talk about and really shouldn't be written in books.

You will understand clearly the deepest and most abstruse philosophers; the cryptic enigmatic sayings of the Illumined Ones of all ages - and the reasons that they spoke so cryptically; you will understand clearly - from within - all the scriptures of all races and religions. And more. For you will be imbibing from the same source - the same mind - the same genius that they went to. Nothing - no, not one single thing, shall be withheld from you.

You will understand the Great Plan and your particular place in it. And in all probability you will become more useful - more effective - on a wider and more real level - than you ever dreamed possible.

For the Power shall call you to "greater service" not less.

You will understand all politics and all religion; all science and all Art; for you will be in contact with Omniscience - a very real Omniscience. A breathtaking and awesome Omniscience. You will understand all so-called "world problems" "from within" and will be shown what you personally can do about it.

But please, don't take my word for it. You are invited to find out for yourself. And if you make "Thy Will Be Done" your number one priority - and "have no other Gods before Me" - at least for the time you are meditating - you WILL find out. You will, definitely and surely experience a Power which is VERY VERY REAL.

2

Clearing Obstructions

"Streams of Joy fill the ocean of the creator's thought. And thou, pouring drops of joy into the human soul, art bringing offerings to the creator of the universe."

"Joy is a special wisdom."

Leaves of Morya's Garden

Introduction

Though these chapters can be read in any order with profit, it seems to me that it is best to read "Part I" before reading the following:

Read the whole chapter through once before starting any of the processes.

Your deeper mind will understand perfectly what it is that you're trying to achieve - and once it gets the idea, will cooperate thoroughly. This, in spite of the fact that your "conscious/everyday mind" may be puzzled.

One of the first things that happens to us when we begin meditating - aside from an initial rush of peace and bliss - is an acute awareness of persistent/troublesome/impish trains of thought. They are especially irksome to us because we have "tasted the bliss - the heavenly honey" and we "want to go back for more - more, more and more". If we've been meditating correctly, we've "touched" - however slightly - "the Kingdom of Heaven" and though the soul may not yet be "abiding there" - might not yet be a "citizen" of that Realm" -

it longs to be. We feel a bit "frustrated" at these mental movements that "tug at us" and seem to obstruct us from our Destination.

Actually, when these "repressions"/angers/dialogues/ arguments/judgments/criticisms/resentments/grievances" come up to your conscious awareness, it's a very good sign and we should be "rejoicing and praising the Power". Yet few of us do.

What is happening is that the Power that you have called on is "coming into its Temple" and beginning to "reclaim it" - to take possession of what "rightfully" belongs to it. And this power will not tolerate any impurities of thoughts or feeling in its temple. It will not tolerate anything that obstructs its "Rapture" and "Will" from expressing itself through its Temple - and so they will go. Go they must - and don't feel sad about this. Most of it is just excess "baggage" - rubbish really. Things that have probably been obstructing you for years and years.

It is "Christ driving the money changers from the Temple of the Body Beautiful". And though the experience is seldom "pleasant" - at least not while it is happening - the end result is always good. It is God Himself "searching the joints and the innermost members" - on the deepest possible levels - clearing and healing and purifying the mind, the deeper consciousness and eventually the body. "Nothing that maketh for a lie" shall remain.

You will not believe at first - it is quite shocking really - at how much "repressed" material we all carry around with us. It is absolutely incredible. And the deeper (or higher) you go in meditation - the more "advanced" you become, the more of it you have to deal with.

The power you have called on is going to "have its way" with you. Make no mistake about it. It is incredibly "willful" and this is true whether or not one meditates. The meditator is just more acutely aware of it. But you can "cooperate with the Power - help it along - work "with it" instead of in opposition to it - understand what it is "driving at" and become part of the process instead of part of the problem. In other words, you can cooperate with the power in "cleaning your temple of mind and body".

As we mentioned, the power can do it alone but if we resist, the process can be very traumatic. Every crisis that occurs to people (whether they meditate or not) is always a result of some conscious or unconscious "resistance to or blockage" to the Divine Life Urge from above.

We can catalogue some of the main resistances/obstructions/barriers to the flow of Spiritual Power/Life Force as follows:

Hatred/Malice - these twin devils must absolutely go and they will go!
Fear/worry/insecurity/doubt
Condemnation, whether it be of oneself or of others
Self-diminishment - of oneself or others
Poverty/Failure/Futility/Frustration
Self-Denial or Denial of Others
Deceit/dishonesty/duplicity/injustice
Confusion
Self-Pity
Jealousy/Envy (these will be transformed into genuine admiration)
Weakness/Inadequacy
Anger (this will take some time but it can be removed and transformed)
Irritation/vexation/annoyance
Disharmony
Ignorance (this is a biggie but the Power is also Omniscient and it knows very well how to cure this condition.)

Depression/Sadness/Grief/Sorrow
Hurt/Pain (very difficult to meditate when you're in pain)
Doubt or disbelief in the Power

When these are removed/eradicated/transformed in a human consciousness - we find the most amazing revelation! GOD! Man Minus the above equals God! But don't take my word for it, hopefully you'll find out for yourself.

There are other things to be dealt with also but we've got enough for a start - enough to keep us busy for quite a while. And its well worth the effort. I can't think of anything more difficult or challenging to do. Nor can I think of anything that is ultimately more profitable and satisfying - on all levels. Everyone of the things listed that is "conquered" or "overcome" will bring an "increase" in life force and well-being - on all levels. And if you persist (and this is not a path for weak/timid people) your life will surely become "magical/miraculous/ wonderful"! And you will have achieved more in terms of REAL POWER than any Caesar or Alexander or Napoleon. For they are only conquerors of the "visible" while we are called on to be conquerors of BOTH the visible and the invisible - of things and forces that no Caesar ever imagined.

Hopefully, you've been keeping a notebook during your meditations. This is important. More important than you can possibly realize at the present. For eventually it will become for you a real magical tool. But for the present you should be jotting down your experiences and feelings during each session. Make special note of any "disturbing thoughts/images/fears/ animosity" that comes up - especially if it is persistent. These are "signals and messages" to you that there are "impurities" in the consciousness. Something is going on "deep down" that you might not be aware of - or that you might not have resolved - or that you might have repressed.

Here is a classic exercise for clearing these bad feelings/

images, etc. I didn't invent this but have used it for many years and it works.

Writing Out Technique

Don't do this exercise if you have to immediately leave your house or drive an automobile or embark on some business that requires your full mental alertness. Do it at times when you know you will have some time to rest afterwards - on a weekend, or at night before retiring.

Get a timer and set it for fifteen minutes.

Get a ream of loose leaf paper and a pen.

Center yourself between the eyes and declare yourself to be "An Immortal Spiritual Being - A Being of Light - One with God and in Perfect Union and Harmony with the Universe."

Take a sheet of paper and on the top write:

"I (followed by your name) am now clearing and ridding myself of all negative/undesirable/malicious thoughts and feelings about (and here write down one of the disturbing topics/images that has been bothering you in meditation - it could be some person you're angry with - or some memory of something that was done to you long ago - or some situation that you fear or hate or feel frustrated with - the topic doesn't really matter.)

Now start to write out all that you think and feel about the situation. Write out what happened. Write out your anger. Write out your hatred. Write out your hurt and pain and grievance. Don't hold anything back. Get angry. Get upset if you like. But get the emotional charge out on the paper. Do this until your timer rings. Then (and this is important!) WITHOUT REREADING WHAT YOU HAVE WRITTEN, either tear the pages to shreds or burn them.

As you do this you should think and feel that you are "ripping and burning" these thoughts and feelings from your subconscious. You might want to say out loud - These thoughts and feelings are removed and eradicated from my consciousness now and forever. Amen."

Your "deeper mind' will get the idea (especially if you make a regular practice of this) and will joyfully respond. The person/situation/fear or whatever will cease to trouble you.

When you go back to your meditation you will find that you are "unblocked/unburdened" and the spiritual force will come through stronger.

Do this exercise for every topic or train of thought that troubles you in meditation. In most cases you will find that these things were not only troubling you in meditation but in life as well. And as they are "cleared and discharged" that particular life-difficulty will also "magically and mysteriously and effort-lessly" be resolved.

Please Note: Most of these repressions/angers/condemna-tions/opinions and negativity are considered "garbage". They are considered to be little more than "psychic excrescences" and you would no more take these things back inside of you (by rereading what you've just written/excreted) than you would take back physical excrescence. Its the same thing on another level.

Some people find it helpful to keep a pillow nearby when they do this exercise so that if they get "really angry they can kick, punch, beat or stamp on it and thus express their anger in a physical way. This is okay but remember when the timer rings, stop and get back to your meditation.

Taping Exercise

This is a variation on the "writing out technique". Some people get better results by "talking it out" while others get better results by writing. These things are a matter of temperament. You might want to alternate between the two ways - one time do the writing out and the next time do the taping.

The procedure is basically the same except that now you are using a tape recorder and a blank tape - a cheap 30 minute cassette will do nicely. Set your timer for fifteen minutes.

Declare yourself to be who you are - "An Immortal Spiritual Being - A Being of Light - One with God and in Perfect Union and Harmony with the Universe".

Say out loud - into the tape - "I will and desire to rid, clear and remove these thoughts and feelings from my consciousness."

Then talk out your feelings/thoughts/animosity/venom or whatever into the tape recorder. Tape it. But DON'T REPLAY THE TAPE.

When you are done, rewind the tape and erase it. As you erase it, say out loud (and feel inside) "These thoughts and feelings are NOW erased from my consciousness, just as they are erased from the tape."

Then go back to your meditation. You will find that the power comes through smoother and stronger.

These things that you are "outing" with these exercises have been lurking in your consciousness for years and years, clogging up the "works". It's wonderful to get rid of them. And these are safe ways to do it.

Since these things (until the clearing work is done) are "vibrating" in the consciousness - you have been (as we all have been) unconsciously "projecting" these "disharmonies" into the Divine Mind - and onto other people - many of whom you say that you love. These disharmonies have been hurting those you love and of course - ultimately - have echoed back to you. Isn't it wonderful that its now - gradually - being reduced".

You'll find as you continue with these processes (and they are processes, their effects are cumulative over time) that you have less of a need to "dump" your negativity on your friends/lovers or acquaintances - many of whom subconsciously resent you for doing that - though they may not say it to you. To the contrary you will soon be in a position to either lift them up or project positive and constructive vibrations to them. You will become more popular - more magnetic - more charismatic - more dynamic - which presents a whole new set of challenges. But still it is better than the previous condition.

Reducing the amount (never mind the total elimination - that will take time) of psychic pollution that we emanate is every person's personal responsibility - as you will find out as you continue your meditations. For you are totally responsible - and the "Supreme Being that you worship (under whatever name that you worship it) will hold you responsible for your "psychic emanations". Life holds us responsible. It's in the nature of things. So what you're doing is ultra important not only for your own personal welfare, but for the personal welfare of everyone you hold dear and all those around you as well. It's a patriotic and constructive use of the will and use of your time and energy.

There is nothing surer to obstruct or detune you from the Spiritual Power than hatred or malice. It not only detunes you from your "Source" but causes many other personal/relationship and health problems as well. These two things are deadly psychic poisons. And should be thought of that way. As you continue your meditations you will definitely know that your God is benevolent - that benevolence is its very essence and nature and it could not contain within itself anything unlike itself. So if you find yourself hating someone - no matter how justified you think this hatred is - be careful. You're out of tune. Here's a method that will clear out these feelings and put you back in "alignment" or in "tune" with the Power.

A Technique for Clearing Hatred/Malice/Resentment

Think of the person that has hurt you - whom you hate - whom you are angry with. Get a clear picture in your mind. Then from your "Immortal I Am" say to the person (or group of people) "Neither do I judge thee. Neither do I condemn thee. Neither do

I accuse thee. Neither do I resent thee." Repeat this over and over again - like a mantra. Every time that person (or group) comes to your mind, repeat the statement to it.

The most amazing things will happen when you practice this. First off, you will feel a "release" - the higher power will start to come though again. And this is the most important phenomena. You're back "in tune and alignment". You have regained "access to your Genius" and are therefore in a good position. Secondly, the relationship with the people that you've been saying this to will also undergo dramatic change. Sometimes there's reconciliation - in very dramatic ways. Sometimes there is a "parting of the ways" - but it will be very harmonious and "painless". And sometimes you will see a need to "stop their activities" - and this is o.k. - especially if they are not spiritually evolved and just don't know any better and can't help doing the hurtful/malicious things that they're doing. If the third course becomes necessary you will easily be able to stop them since you will not be "hating" them. You will be able to do "what is necessary" in the most compassionate and cosmic way - without any vengeance/hatred or malice in your heart or mind. Or, you will see ways - ways will be revealed to you by your Higher Genius - of protecting and shielding yourself from their malicious vibrations and activities. There are no rules. But if there's no hate or malice in your heart and you're coming from "Thy Will be Done" - you will always do the right thing.

The above technique can also be used with habits you don't like - or with things about yourself that you don't like - whether it be your physical appearance - or some physical feature - or some unease of body or mind. Say to it - over and over again - Neither do I judge Thee. Neither do I condemn Thee. Neither do I accuse Thee. Neither do I resent Thee. The condition will cease to have any "power over you" - will cease to have power to obstruct your thought or attention - will cease to have power to trouble you or cause you pain. It is absolutely incredible!

If you do it with people, those people will cease to have any power to hurt or harm you. For you will be in a position of "clarity" - "tuned in" and you will know long beforehand whether you need to take protective measures. You will also be in a position to get true and accurate "guidance from Above" as to how to best handle the situation.

3

More Techniques for Clearing Obstructions

"Neither Caesar, not the world, not the mortal condition is evil, my beloved. Caesar wills only to conquer the visible; the world is as men have willed it to be; and the mortal condition is but an illusion. Those who will may stay there until such time as they unwill. But my teaching offers possibilities - choices - options - alternatives. And this is the primary virtue. Ye need not be limited by the world; ye need not be bound by material conditions; or be slaves of Caesar; or subject to the wills and judgments of mortals - though ye will render unto each what is rightfully theirs. Thy soul is greater than all of these and thy soul hath choice. Ye can choose between happiness and unhappiness; between harmony and disharmony; between the land of milk and honey and the putrid stench of human hells. I offer thee choice. I offer thee opportunity. Thy soul is a vast empire and ye need not dwell in the swamps therein."
The Magic Stone

Hopefully you have become proficient in the rituals described in Chapter 2. Don't ignore them as they have other - more advanced - wonderful uses. And we'll deal with them later on.

Hopefully you're beginning to see that the main objective of these exercises is to turn the Power back on. Clearing the clogging and the jamming so that the Original Spirit - the true Will of your Genius - can flow through its normal and appointed channels. When this occurs we can consider whatever problem we have as solved. It always works through an alteration of our consciousness - then and only then do conditions change.

Let us say that you are having some problem in visualizing

the bubble of light spoken of in Chapter 1 - or that you have some trouble in visualizing the material thing that you spoke the word for - or some person in the office is giving you a hard time and disturbing your inner peace or tranquility. It doesn't matter what it is. Perhaps it's some obsessive fear - or nightmare. Whatever it is, you can clear it either with the rituals given in Chapter 2 or with the following exercise given to me by my teacher (you can have his name on request) and for which I'm eternally grateful.

Touch and Let Go Technique

Procedure

Get a pencil (make sure it's a pencil, this is important) and some blank paper.

On the paper, in pencil, write out the name of the person who is disturbing you - or the image that is disturbing you or the *formless* fear or feeling that obstructs your ability to contact your divinity - or obstructs your power to visualize what you will to visualize. Write it down on the paper.

Set your timer for 15 minutes. And, again, don't do this if you have to rush off somewhere in the outer world - or when you are going to drive a car - or do anything where you need full mental alertness. Make sure you have from one to two hours to rest afterwards.

Center yourself between the eyes (this space by the way is about as high as we can go and still be called a human being - anyone centered or established above that point - say over the head - is not really human anymore but MORE than that!) And declare that, "I Am An Immortal Being of Light, At One with God and in Perfect Union and Harmony with the Universe."

Then say, "In the name of the Wisdom, the Love, the Justice and the Mercy of the one eternal Spirit it is my will and desire to clear, cleanse and neutralize myself of any undesirable thoughts or feelings on these subjects. So mote it be."

This is sort of a *declaration of intent* to your deeper mind (and to other invisible forces) who will be cooperating with you. It also helps you to focus.

Now touch the paper - the names or the images that you have written on it - and let it go. Touch it and let it go. Touch and let go. Get into a nice, easy, relaxed rhythm. Touch and let go. Repeat. Repeat. Repeat. Do this for 15 minutes and then stop.

Write down your experiences, your feelings - any images or memories - or insights - or physical reactions that occurred in your notebook. This is very important!

Then go back to THY WILL BE DONE as described in Chapter 1. (Or any other of the exercises that you might be doing.) The Power should flow in much easier and smoother and more abundantly. There will be more light in your aura - more clarity in your mind - more power to your thought and your will.

This exercise should be repeated as necessary. In the beginning though, it is not recommended that you do it more than once a day and not more than 15 minutes per session.

This exercise not only has a psychological effect but also seems to work on the deepest of the cellular memory. Every cell of the body is in reality a *unit of mind* - a little mind - a piece of your overall consciousness. Every trauma, fear, shock that the mind has ever experienced is recorded in the appropriate cells. We tend to experience different emotions in different parts of the body. This exercise will work on the cell consciousness. So that if the body must again face a similar image, person or experience it will be calmer, more relaxed, more tuned in to the Higher Intelligence.

Do you feel depressed? What was the image or situation that depressed you? Try to catch the exact image. Write it down and do some *Touch and Let Go* on it. It will clear.

Did someone say something that hurt you? Upset you? Scare you? What was the word? Write it down and do some *Touch and Let Go*. Those words will cease to have any negative impact on you and you will be able to deal with the situation rationally, positively and in the most effective way.

Touch and Let Go is just as effective with groups of images as it is with one or two images. Let's say there are five or six, or even more things or images that disturb you. Write them down and do *Touch and Let Go* on the whole bunch of them.

You will feel indescribably better. You will feel releases - snaps, givings, shiftings of your body and mind. It's wonderful. You will be more in control and more able to visualize clearly what you want in your auric sphere and more in tune with the Higher Power when it flows into you.

Your memory and logical powers will also improve steadily and gradually. There was never anything really wrong with them - they were just clogged up.

There is yet another technique for clearing out the clogging and jamming. This system or method, *Command Phrase Technique*, was pioneered by Richard C. Wetherill. He wrote a number of books on the subject (one of them being *Truth Is Power*), most of which (to my knowledge) are out of print[1] But if you ever have a chance to get a copy - get it. His work is clear, workable and beautiful.

His main thesis is that any problem or difficulty that a person has, stems from some "basic distortion of logic" caused by a "command phrase" that WE ourselves installed - or accepted - during periods of intense emotion - anger, fear, pain, etc. We made a statement that we knew to be *untrue* - illogical. We said it in a moment of anger or passion and then we forgot about it when the emotion subsided. This phrase or phrases however were installed or programmed into the subconscious (which never forgets and which always acts on every command that we give to it) and thus a problem or difficulty was created.

It is very easy to locate negative command phrases and clear them.

Take any problem that you might have. A persistent problem. Sit down and start writing out your thoughts about it. All kinds of command phrases will instantly leap up. They were there all the time - operating - silently and secretly in your deeper mind because your deeper mind thought that you wanted it there. After all you did speak the word - you did *command it* - and what else could it do but obey you?

Since we're dealing with meditation we'll deal with some of the common negative command phrases on this subject - but keep in mind that the principle applies to any subject that you're interested in - and can be a powerful tool in any area of life that you want to improve.

I CAN'T MEDITATE.

Are you sure? Do you know that everybody meditates without exception? That is, everybody has a dominant focus of interest - something that they give undivided attention to. The only issue is on WHAT do they meditate. Some people are meditating on their problems, their own personal hells. Others - notably businessmen - meditate on money and profits. Everybody meditates on something. Even you who say that you can't meditate.

I NEVER HAVE TIME TO MEDITATE.

Really now, never?

I CAN'T FOCUS. I CAN'T CONCENTRATE.

Are you sure? Wouldn't it be more correct - more true - to say that *some* times there is more difficulty in focusing than others?

GOD IS DEAD. THERE IS NO GOD.

Well, if you keep talking like that you certainly will never experience it.

MEDITATION DOESN'T PAY THE BILLS.

Who told you that one!

MEDITATION IS FOR WEAK PEOPLE.

Boy, are you going to learn something!

MEDITATION DOESN'T WORK.

Well, if you hold on to that it won't work! And if you said that about the medicine that your doctor prescribed for you, that wouldn't work either!

Hope you see what I'm driving at here.

There are literally thousands upon thousands of these impy, negative phrases floating around in our minds - either which we ourselves have installed or which come to us through the influence of the *collective mind* (which is a whole other subject too big to be dealt with here - but which you will find out about if you keep on meditating).

Command Phrase Technique
Procedure

In your magical notebook (and it will become magical to you - a true tool of magic) make note of your negative phrases. List as many as you can.

Center yourself between the eyes and declare yourself to be "An immortal Being of Light, At One with God and in Perfect Union and Harmony with the Universe" - and that you are interested in living by what is ABSOLUTE RIGHT AND ABSOLUTE TRUTH.

Give each of the phrases some conscious attention. Look at them from the viewpoint of your IMMORTAL SELF. Note how false and untrue these statements are. And even if some of them contain some germ of truth, note how distorted and misleading the phrase is. Ask yourself is it *definitely* true? Is it *maybe* true? Is it true at certain times and not at others? Is it *absolutely* true? As you do this and see the fallacy of these things they will automatically release. You will also get the memory and the emotion that you had when you originally installed them. Were you trying to be cute? Humorous? Trying to impress someone? Were you angry? Trying to get someone riled or upset? Whatever it was, you will see why you made the statement and that it was not *absolutely* true and its power will be released from the subconscious.

You can actually feel the command phrase *give* when you do this.You can physically and mentally sense the release.When you do, you can stop with that phrase and go to the next one. Keep doing it until all of them are released. It's great fun and rewarding.

Another technique, *Casting the Burden,* is a technique taught in many metaphysical schools and it works almost always - actually it always works - but it sometimes leads to unexpected solutions.

Casting the Burden Technique
Procedure
Think of your problem or whatever seems to be obstructing your meditation - no matter what it is - and say, "I cast this burden of (and then name the problem - fear, financial worry, hatred towards so and so, my relationship with so and so, the $10,000 that I need, the pain in my shoulder, or whatever) upon the God within (under whatever name you choose to call Him) and I go free."

Repeat this a few times. Very often the release is instantaneous and dramatic - you can feel the problem dissolving instantly. Sometimes the solution appears a bit later on. But every time the troubling problem comes to your mind just repeat the statement: "I cast this burden (then name it) upon the God within and I go free in harmony."

The beauty of this technique is that you don't have to be at home in a meditative state to do it. You don't need tools or paraphernalia to do it. You can do it anywhere at anytime.

4

Color Meditation

*"Ye who attack BEAUTY beware! Ye slander not only the Most
High but the entire creation as well. Rest assured that the creation
which IS Beauty in essence and substance and which was created by
Beauty will have its revenge. Though I myself am far from understanding the Ultimate Purposes of the Great Beauty, there are those
who are Greater than I who say that Beauty IS the ultimate purpose
of the creation. I am not in a position to either affirm or deny this
but am inclined to agree. It `rings true' in my soul."*

The Magic Stone

This is a BIG subject and again we'd like to make it clear that
there is no pretense of presenting the "one and only true way"
for using color. We're only presenting ONE workable method.

Color therapy or meditation (and on its deeper more advanced
levels it could be called "Agni Yoga" - the Yoga of Fire) is an area
where we find almost no consensus among different practitioners. The student is literally inundated with a plethora of
systems, each of which seems to contradict the other. This does
not negate the Science of Color - nor the positive healthful
benefits that Color meditation bestows on its practitioners. It only
indicates to us that the Yoga of Color is a VERY PERSONAL
MATTER, and that different colors affect different people differently - and affect the same person DIFFERENTLY AT DIFFERENT
TIMES!

This is a very demonstrable and experiential fact - as you will
find out if you practice this.

Color meditation has the power of "breaking" any emotional
state - any depressed or negative state of mind; of purging the

mind of undesirable thoughts and feelings; and of "building" into the character "qualities" that we might be deficient in. It's sort of like taking "spiritual vitamins".

Procedure

You can practice this sitting down, lying down or standing, as you prefer. It works equally well in almost any posture. Select a posture that's comfortable for you.

Center yourself between the eyes and say, "I AM AN IMMORTAL BEING OF LIGHT. I AM AN IMMORTAL RAINBOW BEING. I AM ONE WITH GOD AND IN PERFECT UNION AND HARMONY WITH THE UNIVERSE."

Put your attention on your genital area - your sex organs - and visualize yourself in an egg or bubble of ruby red brilliance. Get the color as clear, pure and brilliant as you can. If you have trouble getting the color - what obstructed you? Make note of it as it will be something you'd do "Touch and Let Go" on.

You can either envision yourself in the egg of ruby red brilliance or you can form an image of a treasure chest over-flowing with red rubies with the sun shining through them in your mind's eyes. Now imagine that you are inhaling this Red Brilliance into your lungs. Take deep inhalations of this red brilliance and see it going into your lungs and from there into your bloodstream and into every single cell and organ of your body.

Breathe deeply. See your body glowing with this pure red brilliance. See every cell and organ cleared, cleansed and purified by this pure red brilliance.

Take about six breaths.

If you are doing this correctly you should feel a "red brilliance" streaming through your fingers, palms and feet.

Now put your attention on your "belly button" and visualize yourself in an egg of "electric orange" - as pure and as brilliant as you can get it. Inhale this "orange brilliance" six times, as before.

Put your attention on your solar plexus (this is just under the chest and above the abdomen right where the chest bone ends.)

Imagine yourself in an egg of "yellow diamond brilliance". If you have trouble seeing it around you, think of a chest of yellow diamonds and start inhaling that brilliance into your lungs and from there into the body.

Again do this for six breaths.

Bring your attention up to your heart and imagine yourself in an egg of emerald green. Inhale it into your lungs and body six times, as before.

Now bring your attention up to the throat and imagine yourself in an egg of Sapphire Blue and again inhale this color into your lungs and from there into your bloodstream and into every cell and organ of your body.

Bring your attention up between the eyes and envision yourself in an egg of Indigo Brilliance. (Indigo is the color of the sky at night when the moon is full - it is neither black nor blue but something in between.) Again inhale it for six breaths.

Bring your attention to the top of the head and visualize yourself in a egg of violet light. Again inhale it for six breaths as before.

Bring your attention up to about six inches above your head, envision an egg of Golden Brilliance and again repeat your breathing.

Bring your attention to a foot above your head and envision an egg of White Diamond Brilliance and repeat the process as before.

You have just "fed" your "inner bodies" with all the nutrients/energies that they need and this will naturally reflect itself in your "outer" sense of well being.

While you are in the Diamond Light you might want to do some "Thy Will be done" as described in Part I. The diamond light is an excellent place to "pray or meditate" from. All prayers made in this light are answered "instantly" - for it is a very "refined" energy - though in many cases it takes time for the "denser layers/levels" of the mind (the psychological and physical levels) to "feel/experience" the answered prayer. To those levels "nothing" has happened - apparently. This is very normal. For you have been "praying/meditating" from a level/dimension *above* those coarser levels and the light needs to condense to a more "material" level before those denser layers "experience it".

Note on the Color Meditation

The previous exercise works very well after you've done "Touch and Let Go" or the "Writing out/Taping" rituals. For, in those rituals you have "outed" - gotten rid of - undesirable energies and magnetism, and with the color meditation you are "bringing in" desirable energy. You are replacing the old and the undesirable with the new and the desirable.

However, it also works very well while you are doing touch and let go! Try doing the "Touch and Let Go" ritual (on one subject) while you inhale each of the colors. You will find that you get more dramatic results with certain colors than with others! This is something that you can feel and experience.

After doing your Color Meditation make sure you enter your results/experiences in your notebook. This is very important since, as we mentioned, there is no consensus among different practitioners as to the effects of color. This is something that you are going to have to determine for yourself. So keep notes on how each color affected you and what happened to you during your meditation.

Most authorities seem to agree (and this author concurs) that Red stimulates and excites; that it makes one more "physical", energetic, passionate, sexual, courageous - and if too much red is in the aura the person will tend to be hot tempered, argumentative, rash, impulsive, and violent. Emerald Green definitely stimulates a feeling of Harmony, Love and Romance (as opposed to the physical passion of red) and seems to bestow "social grace". Gold seems to attract money and seems to strengthen the ego and will. Violet and Indigo seem to "cool" one down and violet seems to have the power of "clearing out obstructions and barriers" to our will. The White Light seems to be the "light of Revelation" and in this light nothing can be hidden - everything gets exposed - whatever is in the aura gets revealed. But there's a lot more to all of this and you should be feeling for yourself what each color "does" to you or for you. It's a BIG BIG subject and we're barely getting our feet wet with this exercise.

There are many ways to perform the Color Meditation. I used the image of an "egg" because later on we're going to get into the subject of Psychic Self Defense (a very important subject - and the deeper you go in your studies and work the more of a need you're going to have to master and understand it) and this exercise is meant as a "Prelude" to creating a "rainbow aura". The Rainbow Aura is a very effective defense against malicious/ spiteful vibrations and against most "Spiritual Bacilli".

If you can envision the EGG of the appropriate color around you all well and good. This is most preferable. If you can't you can get equally beneficial results by either forming an image of the Gem of that color in your mind's eye and inhaling the color of the Gem; or you can think of an object of the appropriate color - i.e. a grove of orange trees for the color orange - and inhale the color from the object. You can even obtain a color wheel or sheet from your local paint store and inhale the appropriate color from the sheet - while focusing on the desire.

Some people like to construct elaborate fantasies to get their "desired color". For example, for blue they would imagine themselves on a "Carribean cruise" - cruising on the blue waters with a clear blue sky above them - on this cruise (presumably with their lover beside them) they inhale the blue of the ocean and the blue of the sky. For green they might imagine themselves in this vast green meadow, with fresh dewy green grass - nicely manicured - beneath them. They are lying in this "vast expanse of green" and inhaling the greenness into themselves.

This is done with each of the colors. It's a lot of fun! And it opens up new vistas for the imaginative and creative faculties.

Some people buy candles of all the colors and inhale the color while focusing on the lit candle of that color.

All of this is well and good. All of these methods definitely work. Choose the method that works best for you.

Personally, I prefer the color of gems since the gems seem to produce the purest and most brilliant aspects of the colors.

The important thing is that you start bringing in these healthful and beneficent energies into your personal auric sphere.

If you are familiar with Kabbala you can do the MIDDLE PILLAR RITUAL (as described in Regardie's THE MIDDLE PILLAR and THE ART OF TRUE HEALING) in each of the colors mentioned.

Color meditation can be used as a prelude to prayer; an aftermath to the "outing" rituals; or anytime you feel "tired/down/depressed".

A more advanced technique for color meditation - and a very powerful one - is to identify with the colors. This is perfectly safe to do if you are coming from your IMMORTAL I AM and not your mortal personal self. Declare yourself to be THE IMMORTAL RED RAY OF THE COSMOS, then inhale the color into yourself. Do this for each of the colors/rays. Make note as to how you feel with each "ray" its impact on you personally and on others that you meet while in your "COLOR IDENTITY". If you practice this diligently you will learn many things that cannot be written about.

If you are doing your color meditation faithfully - making it part of your lifestyle - you will understand the Biblical expressions - "Clothed in the Garments of Light and Praise" - "Fed and nourished by the Spirit". You will see for yourself how to "clothe yourself" spiritually and how impossible it is for YOU the IMMORTAL BEING OF LIGHT to ever lack food or adequate clothing.

5

Breathing Meditation

"Every product - human artifact - represents a problem that has been solved."

The Magic Stone

Once again we are dealing with a very big subject and so we'd like to repeat that we make no pretense of presenting "the One and Only True Way" of breathing, or the only way of using the breath. We're only presenting a few out of many, many techniques that work and that will help you solve most of your human problems.

If you've practiced the color meditation in Part 4 you've already seen that you can inhale the energy of colors directly into the body. You've probably also experienced its almost immediate - instantaneous - impact on the physical body.

Now we are going to use the same basic principle but in a different way. We are going to inhale "Abstract Spiritual Ideas/Energies/Forces" into the mind and the body. We are going to build these Desirable Attributes "qualities" into our "personal auric sphere".

We are going to bring "heaven down to earth"; to "materialize heaven" and "spiritualize earth".

In order for you to perform this meditation with the right attitude - from the correct mental space - with the minimum of mental blocks, we need to explain that every desirable STATE OF MIND exists APART FROM and INDEPENDENT OF any material condition or "object".

What we're trying to say is that your ability to "tune into" or contact any STATE OF MIND - or ANY DIVINE IDEA or

PRINCIPLE or FORCE is not determined by the material condition (whatever it is) in which you find yourself. Please give this some thought for it is absolutely true.

Spiritual Ideas/Forces/Powers are OMNIPRESENT - always there - always available - despite the fact that some of us CHOOSE not to accept them or contact them.

The fact that someone may be lying sick in a hospital bed does not at all negate the FACT that the DIVINE IDEA/SUBSTANCE/FORCE/INTELLIGENCE/POWER that we call HEALTH/WELL-NESS/WELL-BEING is *present* RIGHT THERE all the time. And the instant that the so-called "sick person" contacts this STATE/IDEA/POWER, whether of his own accord or through the help of others, he begins to get well.

In fact, we could define disease/sickness as merely a person's temporary inability to contact or "tune into" or accept the IDEA/FORCE of HEALTH.

The fact that a person may be in a "materialized condition" where he cannot pay his bills or meet his obligations (and there are various reasons why this could have happened - each situation is different) does not at all negate the fact that the DIVINE FORCE OF AFFLUENCE or THE CONSCIOUSNESS OF SPIRITUAL AFFLUENCE is there all the time. It has NEVER left him - though it seems to. Somehow or other he got "de-tuned" from it - lost his conscious contact with it - blocked it or allowed others to block him from it. His need is not physical money (though this is what they usually think!) but his contact with the SPIRITUAL FORCE that we call AFFLUENCE. The instant that this is contacted his condition of poverty/lack begins to change. The rate of change depends only on his capacity to receive the energy.

Again, we could define poverty/lack as a state where the person is out of touch with the Omnipresent Consciousness of Spiritual Affluence.

To the 3-dimensional mortal mind - to those who are "materialists" - these are shocking and sometimes infuriating statements. Revolutionary statements. Too good to be true. Nevertheless, they are true and we invite you to find out for yourself - secretly - without fanfare - in the silence and integrity of your own Soul.

One could philosophize for many volumes trying to describe DIVINE IDEAS - their OMNIPRESENCE their ever availability - their independence of any material condition - their power to change any material condition totally and absolutely (given time); we could theorize, hypothesize, debate and argue about these things endlessly and get absolutely nowhere as far as improving our state is concerned - so here is a way for you to check it out for yourself.

Here is a list of some of (not all by any means!) the DIVINE IDEAS - their OMNIPRESENT PRINCIPLES or ATTRIBUTES. These should cover any particular problem you may have.

LIFE
LOVE
TRUTH
GOODNESS/EXCELLENCE/PERFECTION
BEAUTY
WISDOM/OMNISCIENCE/INFINITE INTELLIGENCE/
    LIGHT
HEALTH/WHOLENESS/HARMONY/WELL-BEING
    (all aspects of the principle of WHOLENESS)
STRENGTH/POWER/OMNIPOTENCE/INFINITE
    DYNAMISM
WEALTH/AFFLUENCE/SUPPLY
JUSTICE
COMPASSION
GLORY
VICTORY/SUCCESS/INVINCIBILITY
RAPTURE/JOY/BLISS/HAPPINESS/FELICITY
PEACE

Procedure

Select any one of the above PRINCIPLES/ATTRIBUTES (based on what you think you need at the present moment. If you feel a financial lack, choose the Wealth Principle; if it is love you think you lack, choose the Love Force; if you're feeling weak/sick or inadequate, choose either Strength or Health.)

Center yourself between the eyes and declare yourself to be who you are: "I AM AN IMMORTAL BEING OF LIGHT, AT ONE WITH GOD (AND THEREFORE AT ONE WITH ALL OF HIS ATTRIBUTES AND QUALITIES) IN PERFECT UNION AND HARMONY WITH THE UNIVERSE."

Envision your Aura of White Diamond Light around you and say firmly that NOTHING MALICIOUS OR DESTRUCTIVE OR DISRUPTIVE MAY ENTER ME OR EMANATE FROM ME.

Let's say that you have chosen LOVE as your topic:

From your IMMORTAL I AM say, "I AM INHALING DIVINE LOVE". Then take a deep breath - imagine that you are inhaling this love force into your lungs and from there into the body. As you breathe out say, "IT IS ESTABLISHED IN MY FLESH".

Do this for 5 minutes in the morning and 5 minutes before retiring.

It should also be done anytime you start feeling "hatred" toward someone or some condition.

This is the beauty of this kind of meditation. It can be done anywhere at anytime - silently, secretly, without any paraphernalia or hoopla.

If this is practiced regularly you will totally transform your personal auric sphere. Your psychic emanations will totally change and so will your life, your relationships and your "outer circumstances.

The 5 minutes recommended time is only a guideline when it comes to this meditation. You may, at times, want to do it longer - and if you are practicing this correctly (It takes a little while to get the hang of it) you will definitely WANT to do it longer - all day and all night. The feeling, the energy is so beautiful. Its impact on others is so beautiful. It will take discipline and "willpower" to "bring you down" from it.

But you will definitely SEE/KNOW/EXPERIENCE what we are talking about previously - that LOVE is an IMPERSONAL DIVINE ATTRIBUTE/FORCE/PRINCIPLE - TOTALLY INDEPENDENT and APART FROM any so-called OBJECT OF LOVE or any MATERIAL CONDITION. And that bringing LOVE into the aura CHANGES the material circumstances.

You will start - little by little - to get a truer, more cosmic perspective on LOVE. You will see and know - no matter what your mother or grandma told you - that you can experience love anywhere at anytime. That it is ALWAYS with you; that you can experience it in a slum or a mansion with equal ease; that material conditions are simply NOT a factor as far as the LOVE FORCE is concerned; that even SPACE AND SO-CALLED TIME are NOT factors as far as the DIVINE ATTRIBUTES/ PRINCIPLES/FORCES are concerned.

You will see that LOVE (like Wealth or Rapture) is not something we get FROM the world - but just the opposite. Its something we RADIATE INTO the world. We "channel" it into the world and by the karmic law (the natural reflexive action of the Universe) the world behaves accordingly - it returns it to us - and so it seems to us that LOVE comes to us from EVERY-WHERE.

This change in perspective (for we are so accustomed to trying to get love and happiness *from* the world, *from* others; wresting it from an apparently "unwilling" world almost by force; through almost every deceit, duplicity, ruse and ploy one can think of) will totally revolutionize your inner and outer life. Love will become as natural to you - as normal for you as "breathing" - no big deal about it.

If you persist in this meditation you will definitely see that what we call "Romantic Love" is only one form of expression of this TITANIC FORCE we call LOVE. And that LOVE comes from "Over the Head" THROUGH the body - not *from* the body; THROUGH the heart, not *from* the heart!

This kind of meditation leads one - if one chooses - and there are many who do choose this - into the "Yoga of Love" - a union with that DIVINE ATTRIBUTE. A beautiful Yoga but very difficult and demanding. (The ones talking "about it" are usually NOT the ones living and practicing it! The ones "living it" are usually too busy to waste time arguing and debating about it!)

This union is achieved (if we may use this word - it is not something we achieve, but "realize". For it is already so on the Soul level) through IDENTITY with the Divine Attribute.

The breathing exercise will lead you to IDENTIFYING with DIVINE LOVE which is a more advanced technique.

Say to yourself, over and over - like a mantra - I AM THE DIVINE ATTRIBUTE OF LOVE - I AM DIVINE LOVE - I AM IMMORTAL LOVE - I AM RADIATING THROUGHOUT THE ENTIRE UNIVERSE.

If you have an argument with your Spouse; your boss just denied you your well deserved raise; your boyfriend/girlfriend is running around with others and you feel like "dying inside" - nevertheless, I AM DIVINE LOVE - DIVINE LOVE KNOWS HOW TO HANDLE THIS - LOVE IS FLOWING THROUGH MY CONSCIOUSNESS - THERE IS NOTHING ELSE I CAN BE!

As we mentioned, the Yoga of Love is very difficult and demanding! And is MOST DEFINITELY NOT for weak people. It's a daily, moment by moment thing. A moment by moment lifestyle.

We have been discussing this exercise in terms of the LOVE force, but it is equally effective with any of the other PRINCIPLES/ATTRIBUTES/IDEAS that we listed previously. The same technique and methodology applies to any of them.

Choose your "favorite" Divine Attribute - the one that appeals to you the most - breathe it in and breathe it out. Eventually (if you choose to carry it that far) you can IDENTIFY with it - and actually become that FORCE/ATTRIBUTE in incarnation.

Make note of who or what "obstructed or denied" you in your meditation. Make a note of it in your diary and when it is convenient, do some "touch and let go" on it, as described in Part 3.

Also make note of whatever else happens during your meditation.

This breathing meditation is actually going to change the physio-chemical-molecular structure of your body - raise the vibrations of your body - purify it - make of it a stronger instrument for radiating and receiving whatever force you're meditating on. So take it easy and give yourself time for the adjustments to take place.

It is also going to lead you - definitely and surely - to "personal revelations" from your Genius. New knowledge - unpublished knowledge - knowledge that couldn't (and perhaps shouldn't) be written down - will be revealed to you. Knowledge that is for "Your eyes only" - meant specifically for you and your personal progress.

And this is the sole purpose of the exercises that we are giving here. They are meant merely to "start you off" - to lead you to the fountain of your own "revelation" which will certainly be different than my revelation or John Smith's revelation - though not in essence or substance - but in specifics.

Therefore, you are always going to know what steps to take next - what YOU personally need to do and should do.

Additional Notes on Breathing

Some people prefer (and I'm one of them) to focus on ALL the Divine Attributes/Qualities/Principles/Forces, rather than just one of them. You can do this by taking a Principle a week (or a principle a month) and work with that exclusively for that period. Over a year's time you will gain a knowledge/experience/ understanding of ALL of them. And it will be a deeper, more fundamental knowledge than anything that you could "read about" in a book.

If you are familiar with Astrology you can choose your principle according to the Transits of the Sun, Moon and planets. Love meditations, for example go much easier (and more powerful) when the Sun or Moon (or both) are in Taurus, Libra or Pisces. Wealth meditations go much easier when the Sun or Moon are in Taurus, Capricorn or transiting your second house. This kind of timing will "boost" the power of your meditation and heighten the experience.

If you are familiar with Kabballa you can chant the DIVINE NAME while inhaling the Principle - the Divine Name that corresponds to the Principle/Attribute that you're working on. The results are very dramatic.

Some people (and there's nothing wrong with this) have trouble thinking about an "Abstract/Impersonal/Principle" - and in truth it IS very difficult for the "Psychological consciousness" to grasp this kind of thing. If you are one of these you might try looking at an IMAGE that encapsulates (as far as you're concerned personally) or embodies the principle that you're working on. This is a very ancient technique.

Let's say that the Love Principle (in your mind) could be symbolized by a man and a woman walking hand in hand along a secluded beach at sunset. Either get a "physical photograph" of this (clip it from a magazine) or image it in your mind's eye. As you look at it, inhale Divine Love.

To many, the Attribute/Force of Divine Love is symbolized by Jesus or Krishna. Those people would look at a physical photograph or artistic rendering of these beings and then inhale Divine Love - as we described in the previous exercise.

To others, the image of the Madonna holding a child in her arms, is the perfect image for Divine Love. Those people would look at such an image - focus on it - while doing their breathing.

The image that you choose is a very PERSONAL matter.

Really, it's a matter of temperament - and one's astrological configuration has a lot to do with it. Choose the image that BEST EMBODIES the Principle/Force/Attribute to your mind.

The use of a "KEY IMAGE" can be used with everyone of the DIVINE ATTRIBUTES that we listed. It's a lot of fun to research and find the one that "does it for you" - the one that "puts you right there" - that makes your soul leap with recognition.

Those who are familiar with the Tarot understand this technique very clearly.

I have found (for me) that the breathing exercise works equally well with or without an image. But you will need to do some personal experimenting for yourself. I have found (for me) the "speaking of the word" - the statement that I AM INHALING PEACE or LOVE or LIFE is sufficient. I have also found that the speaking of the word - leads to the finding of the Perfect Key image of the Force - usually very quickly - sometimes within hours. Then you can decide whether you want to use or dispense with it.

6

The Power of Sound

"The Lord hath given us a sound mind and a sound body. All else is illusion."
The Magic Stone

We'd like to add another potent tool to your arsenal of Spiritual Powers, but again it's important for you to understand that this is another of those, BIG, MAMMOTH subjects. There are many styles, philosophies, approaches and techniques to the use of sound and ALL of them probably work to a degree.

Our task is to find a system that will work for us personally.

So we are going to start simply, with three fundamental sounds: AUM (pronounced OOOHHHMMM, I.A.O. (pronounced EEEE AHHHHH OHHHHH) and the five vowel sounds AHHH EHHHH EEEEE OHHHH UUUUUU.

Procedure

For one week - for about 45 minutes to an hour a day (the longer you do the chanting the more dramatic the result you will get) do one of the chants by itself.

For example, week 1 you may elect to do the AUM; week 2 you might go to I.A.O., week 3 the vowels. The order is not important for now. Choose one chant that appeals to you and work on it for a week.

Center yourself between the eyes and say, "I AM A IMMORTAL BEING OF LIGHT AT ONE WITH GOD AND IN PERFECT UNION AND HARMONY WITH THE UNIVERSE."

Then start your chant. Get into a nice relaxed easy rhythm with it. Inhale deeply and do the chant on the exhalation.

You can chant out loud (if circumstances permit - I personally have not always had this luxury) or mentalize the chant - chant it to yourself inwardly and inaudibly. Either way works equally well except that chanting out loud seems to have a more dramatic impact on the PHYSICAL ORGANISM than chanting inwardly does.

Write down your experiences in your Magical Diary.

Week 4 should be devoted to a combination of all three chants.

I have found the sitting posture best for doing chants - especially if one is chanting out loud for long periods. If you chant while lying down the tendency is to fall asleep.

Notes on Chanting

It is good to chant after you've done the "outing rituals" described in Parts 2 and 3. Also as a prelude and adjunct to "Thy Will Be Done".

For example, while you're in your "bubble of White Light" and asking that the Will of Your Divinity be done you might want to take one of the chants mentioned here and make it a part of your meditation.

Example

"THY WILL BE DONE. OOHHMMMMMMMMMM. THY WILL BE DONE. OHHHMMMMMMMMM."

Or;

"THY WILL BE DONE. AHH EHHH EEEE OHHHH UUUUU. THY WILL BE DONE. AHHH EHHHH EEEEE OHHH UUUU."

Repeat this over and over again for the length of your communion.

You will get amazing results.

You might want to link you chant with some positive affirmation - e.g. I am Healthy, Wealthy and Happy. Ohhmmmmmmmmm. And repeat it over and over again. This is very effective - much more than just an affirmation by itself.

A more advanced technique is to Identify with the chant while doing the chant. For example, "I Am the Immortal OHMMM. OHMMMMMMMM.: or "I Am the I.A.O. EEEE AHH OHHHH". One actually BECOMES the sound - the power of the chant - the vibration of the sound. Difficult to describe. You must do it to understand it.

Whether you use the sound/chant in conjunction with your meditation or just by itself you will get very beneficial results. The sound itself seems to "harmonize" the entire being, all the vehicles, it clears out obstructions/energy masses on the different levels and puts one in a state of euphoria without drugs or alcohol.

Chanting also speeds up the "purification" process - brings up the "impurities" - hatred/malice/anger/condemnation/jealousy etc. and clears them out. It realigns the "molecules" of the body. It "tunes" the whole mind and body to a more "harmonious" pitch.

When the chanting is done correctly you should feel a sense of euphoria and a kind of "Humming Harmony deep, deep within." A humming harmony in the body - in the cells. When this happens you know that you're "in tune" - the Divine Will is working through you unobstructedly and you can relax and enjoy life and whatever you have to do.

Try an hour of chanting when you feel hurt, angry or depressed. It's simply amazing.

Isn't it wonderful! You are no longer a "victim" of your moods but the total and absolute master of them.

These chants can also be used to acquire material things - if you so desire. It doesn't matter what the "thing" happens to be. It doesn't matter how "seeming expensive" or "unattainable" it seems to be. It doesn't matter whether you're asking for a million dollars or for your next meal - the power within - released by the chant will supply it, easily, effortlessly and without stress or strain.

Procedure

Center yourself between the eyes and declare yourself to be who
you are "I AM AN IMMORTAL BEING OF LIGHT, ONE WITH
GOD AND IN PERFECT UNION AND HARMONY WITH THE
UNIVERSE. I AM SPEAKING THE WORD FOR (NAME THE
OBJECT OF YOUR DESIRE - ALSO SEE IT AS CLEARLY AS
YOU CAN) AND I FEEL, KNOW AND BELIEVE THAT I HAVE
IT NOW!

Then chant. Either of the chants that we are using will work
equally well.

"I have my (name object of desire) Now! Oohhhmmmmmm.
Ohhmmmmmm. Ohhhmmmm. My (name the object) is present
with me here and now! Ohhmmmmmmmm. Ohhhmmmmmmmm.
[2]Ohhmmmmm. I have my (name object of desire) now!
OOhhmmmmmm. Oohhmmmmmmm. OOhhmmmm."

Work like this until you feel the "telltale `click' of attainment."
Repeat that you have the thing and chant. When you feel the
"click" - something inside "gives and releases" - that's the signal
that you can stop for the day.

Repeat this form of meditation (or "mental treatment") until
you actually "get" the thing.

If it's something small - something within your "sphere of
availability"[3] - you'll get it very quickly. Sometimes the same
day. Usually within a week.

If it is something big and complicated it might take longer.
But if you repeat this process every day you will attain to it
sooner or later. Moreover, you will be shown - either by inner
revelations, or through "outsiders" - more powerful ways to
work to get the desired thing. You will be shown the "physical
steps" necessary - or the Spiritual steps necessary - for the
attainment of your desire. If it is necessary for you to receive a
whole Spiritual Dissertation on the Subject - you WILL receive it.
The Power will withhold nothing from you.

7

The Magical Diary

"Ye say to me, `who are you to commune with the Most High' - only Prophets, Priests and consecrated One are so permitted. And I say to you, who are YOU to deny me that privilege."
The Magic Stone

Many writers and teachers talk about the usefulness of keeping a record of one's experiences in meditation. There is nothing really new about this. And yet, as far as we're concerned, nothing is useful or useless; no rule or practice is especially sacred or unsacred - no matter how sacrosanct the source - no matter how much we revere the source - until we ourselves have proven it *for* ourselves and *by* ourselves.

This is not meant to demean or dishonor these great teachers, Adepts and Saints. Nor do we mean to promote any kind of irreverence towards them - those who have already MADE the journey that we are only just beginning. But to the contrary, we are only adopting the same attitude that they adopted (had to adopt) in order to get to where they are. If we consulted with them they would (it seems to me) confirm the above statement.

The word of a Master (though it is to be revered - and though we are grateful for it) is still only the word of a Master - an outer, superficial thing - until we demonstrate it in our own personal experience. Then it is no longer somebody's word or teaching but our own living experience. And this is what we're after. Very easy to undermine and sabotage a mere "belief" - there are all sorts of people who specialize in that sort of thing. But very difficult - if not impossible to undermine events/knowledges that have been experienced.

And yet faith is very important...

Getting back to the Magical Diary. This is something that I've practiced on and off. There were periods where my notebook was literally part of my clothing. I would no more walk around without my Magical Notebook than walk around without pants or shoes. And there were periods where I didn't keep one at all. So I guess I'm qualified to say that there's no question about the usefulness and desirability of this wonderful tool of magic. It is especially useful when we start new exercises - venture into unknown "territories of mind".

If you are familiar with Astrology you already know that no two people are quite alike. If you are not familiar with Astrology your particular uniqueness will be revealed to you in other ways. And since you are unique no-one else in the universe is going to experience Meditation in quite the same way that you will. And no-one else in the universe will receive the same revelation that you will receive - though there will certainly be similarities of pattern. YOUR REVELATION - YOUR EXPERIENCE - will always be NEW. Something that's never happened before, and this is probably how you will feel. And though you will respect the revelations of others, you will particularly cherish your own. Therefore you owe it to yourself and to those who will come after you to have a clear record of your experience.

Since your Magical Diary is SECRET - for your eyes only - you have no need to lie. You have the wonderful liberty of being ruthlessly honest - of expressing your true feelings - your true experiences - without fear of offending someone. It is the beginning of real self-expression. And though your self-expression is not yet what it will become - it will expand tremendously in probably undreamed of ways - still it is a beginning. And a beginning is better than nothing.

And since in the beginning there will probably be almost no-one with whom you can discuss your experiences (and this too is wonderful!) it is a nice outlet for that part of the self that needs to "discuss and theorize". Later, you will be grateful for this "gift of privacy".

Thoughts, ideas, intuitions can tend to be very vague and nebulous things if they are not written down. They occur to us at "another" - more rarified level - than we are normally accustomed to. They seem "unreal" to the lower 3-dimensional consciousness and thus they tend to be forgotten rather easily. Writing them down "fixes them" - gives them a "body" - makes them concrete and less likely to be forgotten.

If you have been practicing the rituals and meditations of Part 1 - 6, many, many new ideas and insights have already come to you. You have already been showered with jewels and gems from your higher genius. Write them down. They were given to you for a reason. Many of them contain not only the solution to your present difficulties but also to future ones as well. Though you may not be aware that this is so at the present moment. This has happened to me many times. The solution that I sought was given many months before - it was in my notebook - only I did not realize that it was a solution. Only in glancing through and reviewing my notes did I see what was written - see it in a "new way" - see the hidden import behind it.

Those of you who are scientifically oriented will find that the process of recording your experiences helps you in keeping yourself "objective and detached".

The process of writing and recording your experiences will make you a better observer, communicator and writer.

If you maintain this practice regularly in a year you will have a vast treasury of authentic inner knowledge. Things and techniques that work specifically for you will be revealed to you and you will have access to them via your notes. Eventually - if you choose - you'll be able to write your own course on meditation!

Setting up a Magical Diary is easy. Take any notebook (I like the 9 1/2" x 6" spiral because its small and convenient to carry -

but any size will do) and label it "MY MAGICAL DIARY". Entries should be dated and timed - that is, when you write anything in it make note of the date and the time.

A Sample Entry:

MAY 27, 1998 2:00 A.M.
Did color meditation. Felt warm and good. Felt really dramatic results with the Ruby Red. Something "snapped" - something cleared. But what? It doesn't matter for now. I see a solution for dealing with "X". Wonder if Mr. Y will accept a trade instead of the cash I owe him?? Investigate in the morning.

MAY 23, 1998 NOON
Did OM chanting during lunch break. Not much action for the first ten minutes. After that felt popping in the throat region. After 20 min. started to feel euphoric. My anger towards "Z" dissolved. I know now that everything will work out. Intense memories of fight with father when I was 5 yrs old. Why did that come up? Probably should do some "Touch and Let Go" on it. Make note to do it at earliest convenience. Is there a relationship between my fight with Father and my problem with "Z"?

Your Magical Diary will eventually become your "Private Prayer Book" - your "Personal Bible". And you can use it later on to construct a Magical Treasure Map - another handy and important tool - which we will deal with in Part 8.

The more successful you become - the busier you become - the more you will rely on your Magical Diary to keep tabs and records of all the things that happen to you and all the things that you desire to happen.

8

The Treasure Map

"Ye say ye need `things', and I agree. Ye shall have them, enough and to spare. For ye are entitled to all the best that is in thy spiritual storehouse - to the best that thy consciousness can outpicture for thee. But will ye cheapen me to such a point where 'things' cometh before ME?"
The Magic Stone

If you have been practicing or even reading Parts 1-7 your mind is probably all aboil. There is so much work to be done - so much practicing - so many things to do - so many different techniques - so many skills to learn - and all of this is coupled with your daily responsibilities. In addition you are probably receiving all kinds of new insights - New Practices - variations on the exercises given - specific applications of these exercises geared for your specific needs. Even the biggest mind would tend to feel overwhelmed and confused. What's needed is a way of sorting, sifting, organizing the data; a way of organizing your inner and outer work in ways that are harmonious to you and your lifestyle.

The Treasure Map is one such method. And it's a powerful method. (Again it's not the ONLY method, but it is a workable technique.)

I am not the inventor of this technique. It is taught in most Unity Churches; writers such as Ophiel[4] and Geof Gray Cobb[5] deal with it and many successful business executives use variations on the same theme to organize their minds and achieve goals. Ophiel[6] traces its use back to Ancient Egypt and it is probably even older than that. I have used it and it works.

The Treasure Map is like the programming of a computer.

Except that one programs according to one's own tastes and specifications. It is a way of creating a Master Plan for your life and insuring that your "Deeper Mind" will get the message clearly and act on it harmoniously.

In itself it can be (and is) a form of meditation. One takes a few minutes every day - in the morning and before retiring - to look at it - to "let it sink in" to the mind - to visualize the desires listed there as "present realities in the world of thought" - which they ARE! - to perhaps "speak the word" for their attainment (for those of you who are more metaphysically inclined) - to focus the attention on the positive and constructive rather than on all the things we don't want - to focus the attention on the things that we think will make us happy rather than on the things that are making us unhappy. A very healthy and constructive practice.

The Treasure Map is a sort of centering device to keep our mind on track - the track that we want to travel.

The average person is so bombarded with messages from the collective consciousness - many of which are of questionable value - most of which deal with other people's conception of The Kingdom of Heaven - that its a nice respite to be able to take a few minutes for the contemplation of one's own Kingdom of Happiness and Harmony.

The Treasure Map is an IMPERSONAL TOOL. It can be used for almost anything. Like any tool it can be used or abused. It can be used "positively/constructively/beneficially" or negatively and destructively. It can be used to acquire "material things" - if one so desires - for it was not ordained that we be in a state of "lack". It can be used to attain "spiritual states of consciousness" - closer union with your Divinity - Spiritual Powers or whatever. It can be used to help others. It can be used to help oneself. It can be used to organize and synthesize "outer work" - your work in the world. You can probably use it to hurt others too, if you so desire - but of course you will have to accept the consequences of such a desire - and those are not very pleasant.

THERE ARE NO FORBIDDANCES.

"Your life" says Manly Palmer Hall "is your own personal Mandala". It is your personal work of art. The Treasure Map is the mental plan and design upon which the deeper mind will work and eventually manifest.

Here is your first big test.

How will you design your life? You have Godlike powers over it. Will you create something good, true, beautiful and Cosmic or will you create something ugly and distorted.

Will you use the chart purely materialistically (and that's o.k. if you so desire it) or will you use it spiritually?

I am not here to judge you.

The Treasure Map is basically a Grid - a Matrix - with three columns (see sample), the left column (or Pillar) is for the Will and/or Desire. The Middle column (or Pillar) is for Means and Methods - How you plan, at the moment, to achieve your desire. The right column (or pillar) is for the results.

Procedure

a. You can use the chart supplied above - xerox it - or make your own, according to your personal specs.

b. In the "WILL & DESIRE" column start writing the things or states or goals that you want to achieve.

c. In the "MEANS & METHODS" column write down any ideas or initial hunches of how you think you can proceed to get your desired thing or goal. If you can't think of any way at the moment, that's o.k., as you work with the chart the means and the methods will come to you.

d. Make sure that you date the desire - i.e. note the date (in the box) of when you entered the desire into your Map.

e. In the "RESULT" column enter the things that start to happen in the attainment of your desire or goal. If its a material thing, make note of the date that you received or attained it.

f. Look at the chart/map for a few moments in the morning and for a few moments when retiring. This "activates" the "mental machinery". If you have spare time during the day you can use it productively by contemplating your Map.

g. As you practice this daily contemplation regularly new ideas of attainment - intuitions - will come to you. Don't ignore them. Enter them into your "MEANS & METHODS" column. Some of these might sound "hairbrained", some might sound "reasonable". Put into action the ideas that you CAN implement. The ones that are impossible to implement leave alone for a future time.

h. Very often - and this sounds incredible - you will attain to the thing with no IDEA of how you will proceed. No CONSCIOUS IDEA anyway. But the deeper mind or subconscious knows exactly how to bring it to pass and if it is necessary for you to CONSCIOUSLY understand and cooperate you will "get the signals". If it is not necessary, the subconscious will just "bring it to pass" - for it is connected to the Universal Mind and is (on its deeper levels) "unobstructed" by trivialities such as "space and time and economics etc". I like the analogy of the Computer in this regard - as an explanation. I can use the computer and get very beneficial results from it without much "conscious understanding" of its inner workings. As long as I press the right buttons and execute the command properly the computer will do what it is commanded to do.

i.   Small, simple things will happen very quickly - within hours or days. Bigger things might take some more time - especially if they are not in your "Sphere of Availability" (as Ophiel mentions). - or if the desire or state tends to be "disruptive". However they WILL happen, inexorably, by Cosmic Law.

j.   The Treasure Map can be used with equal effectiveness for Long Term, Medium Term or Short Term goals.

k.   After some experience with this method one gets into a nice relaxed easy rhythm with it. There is no stress or tension in the manifestations. Things happen in a regular and relaxed manner. A point is attained where the Deeper Mind acts on the *ENTIRE CHART* as a *UNIT* - as a Master Plan and the manifestations (or demonstrations) cease to be "on and off" things - disjointed etc. But coherent, regular and all harmonious (provided of course, that you keep your desires constructive and non-malicious).

l.   If you are familiar with Kabballa you can color code your Treasure Map with the color of the Planet/Divine Attribute that rules the thing or activity that you desire. The way to do this is to group similar desires - desires ruled by each planet - on separate charts - each chart of a different color. You can also, if you like, put the appropriate Divine Name on the top of each chart and chant the Name as you contemplate the chart.

m.   Dating of the desires and of the time of attainment is VERY IMPORTANT! After a while you get a clear, concise history of your progress. Very Scientific. It will serve to bolster your faith and understanding of what you are doing - and boy are you ever going to need faith.

n. A more advanced technique is to visualize each "box" in the chart as you contemplate it. Go down your list and make a conscious Mental Image of each thing. Once you get the hang of it you'll be visualizing your entire chart very quickly - in minutes. Do it in the morning and in the evening before retiring - or whenever you have spare time. If something is obstructing your visualizations make a note of it and do some "touch and let go" as described in Part 3. When you get back to your visualizing you'll find it much easier to do.

o. As you progress in this work your Treasure Map is going to undergo radical alterations and changes. This is only normal. Some things will have been attained. New things will have been added. Some desires will get modified. You will probably reach a stage where your Treasure Map is many pages long!

p. Your Treasure Map, like your Magical Diary, is SECRET. FOR YOUR EYES ONLY. Not advisable to go showing it around to people - even your intimates. When the "thing" or "state" is attained they will inevitably find out about it. But in the meantime you don't need to talk. Let your results talk for you. This practice will shield you from a lot of negative vibrations and opposition to your work. There's enough negativity to deal with as it is, we don't need to add to it or make our work more difficult than it already is.

Later on you'll be glad that you kept things secret. I can assure you of that.

Once you see how it is that you get things - how the Mind operates to bring things to you - and how possible it is for you to have your heart's desire - you will probably be confronted with certain Philosophical/Spiritual conundrums; the main one being - What is it that I should desire? There is so much to Be, Do and Have, what shall I choose?

Everyone goes through this and the solution is some long sincere stretches of "Thy Will Be Done" as described in Part 1. When you come down from that kind of meditation it is always with a clarified mind - and this of course, should be your primary desire. Number one on your Magical Treasure Map. Everything proceeds from that.

MAY YOUR MAGICAL TREASURE MAP LEAD YOU - THE READER OF THIS - TO EVERY DESIRE AND EVERY DESIRABLE THING. MAY IT LEAD YOU FROM POVERTY TO POWER; FROM LACK TO ABUNDANCE AND TO THE VERY PINNACLES OF ATTAINMENT.

SO MOTE IT BE!

THE TREASURE MAP

I Will and Desire To	Means & Methods	Results

9

The Power of Praise

"My Son, there are those who seek the Light and there are those who only say they seek the Light. O sharp blade of Truth discern and cleave asunder these two species. The former I cherish. I straighten their path wherever the Destiny permits. To the latter I am a sealed book."
The Magic Stone

Praise is one of the most ancient mental/spiritual laws that we know about. It is written about in all bibles. Teachers teach about it. Writers write about it. Everyone seems to "know" about it but few people really understand it and fewer practice it.

The interesting thing about praise is that we don't really understand it until we do it - until we start practicing it in all the circumstances that confront us.

When we DO it we begin to understand all the ancient mystics, psalmists and gurus. For it is an incredible power. It is the password - the key by which we unlock the gates of the Kingdom of Heaven Here and Now. Through Praise you can enter the Kingdom at will - anytime and anywhere.

The greater your degree of consciousness - the more advanced you become - the greater will be your capacity for Praise. The greater your capacity for praise the more of the Kingdom of Heaven you can manifest.

The power of praise can be applied anywhere at anytime under all conditions. You don't need any paraphernalia to practice it. It is equally effective in a mansion or in a slum; in a hospital bed or in the baseball field; for the rich or the poor. It doesn't matter who you are or what your circumstances may be. Praise is the beginning of the way out.

Praise not only elevates the consciousness; transforms the vibrations; but will also neutralize and nullify the most devastating "attacks of the enemy".

Very often - and I realize that this will sound incredible to some of you - the praise itself is the solution you seek. And in the cases where it is NOT the solution it is definitely the "way to the solution".

Praise is the origin and real meaning of Prayer. It's about the "Highest Form" of prayer that we know about. It ranks on a par (at least in my opinion) with "Thy Will Be Done" which we discussed in Part 1.

It is one of the most powerful and PRACTICAL - FUNCTIONAL and USEFUL - tools that we can acquire. But don't take my word for it. If you work with it - develop the habit of it - you will find this out for yourself.

Praise is also one of the best and most powerful means of Psychic Self Defense that we know about (we are going to go deeper into this subject in future chapters) - it will neutralize - very effectively - almost instantaneously - any kind of psychic attack - and if you are on this path you can expect many psychic attacks. It is an invisible armor which nothing malicious or belittling can penetrate.

It is an incredibly healthy practice to take a half hour a day to quietly and meditatively praise "every crumb of good" in your universe. If your circumstances are so "dire" that you can find nothing to praise - start praising your Divinity (under whatever name you choose to worship it). This by the way is the whole secret revelation of the Psalms. Magical things will start to happen. If you maintain it - keep your mind centered in it - and this is not always easy, though it gets easier with practice - your situation will become totally transformed.

The universe is alive. Everything in it lives. Its essence is spirit and Mind - the very substances and movers of Life. The universe reflects back to you whatever you think and whatever you say. It reflects back to your judgments and secret condemnations. If you belittle your universe you start to live in a "little" stifling kind of universe. It reacts reflexively to praise. Whatever you praise starts to grow and expand - starts to get better. Until - suddenly - "out of the blue" - "like a thief in the night" - you find yourself in your kingdom of heaven. The praise "shatters and demolishes" the mental barriers of lack and limitation - of resentment and grievance - of pain, sorrow and depression. It reveals to you the things that have always been there but which you couldn't see because of the mental barriers you unconsciously created (and there is no condemnation in this for we have all at one time or another been guilty of these things, but let's not waste time thinking about our past mistakes - let's praise our way into the kingdom of our heart's desire.)

If you do some sincere meditation on the Kingdom of Heaven - even from a theoretical/philosophical viewpoint - you will see that it is - MUST BE - a kingdom of praise. It is a Kingdom of the Wonderful and the Fabulous. And this too is implicitly implied in most scriptures of all races. It is a place of ABSOLUTE GOOD - Shambhalla - Eden - the Isles of the Blessed. It is an Eternal Psychological/Spiritual "Inner Space" which we all have access to - and praise is the key to it. Think about the kind of perfection that a Perfect/Unlimited/Omnipotent Mind could create - if it so willed. There could be no "evil" in it - and thus there could be no judgment - no condemnation - no guilt - no unhappiness. What would there be to condemn or judge? What would there be to defend against? To attack?

There would be nothing to do in such a space except to praise and enjoy all the good that one is experiencing.

By getting into the "Praise Frequencies" we are in a sense "appropriating" or "tuning in on" those spiritual spaces. We become resonant to those Minds/Intelligences who dwell there and they - through the medium of our Higher Genius - can reach us - guide us - advise us.

We're getting into areas that are difficult to describe but you will definitely understand it if you practice it.

Very difficult - if not impossible - to feel hateful/malicious/angry or hurt while you are in a state of praise. Impossible to feel fear or jealousy while in a state of praise. Impossible to feel depressed while in a state of praise. Impossible even to feel "poverty/stricken" while in a state of praise - and this was a staggering revelation to me. But again please don't take my word for it. You're cordially invited to try it. The more you do it the greater your capacity becomes.

To those who are materialists[7] (and these people are really the most naive and credulous people imaginable - though they claim to be "realists") this is the utmost absurdity. This attitude to them - the sincere ones - is the height of self-deception - unreality. And then there are those among them who have other motives for their attacks - and we're not talking about those.

This attitude of praise (even though kept secretly in the deeps of the soul) infuriates them, threatens them, bothers them. And perhaps it is right and fitting that it should be so - very understandable - for those people who live in a bleak universe - in psychologically desolate spaces. Your vibrations of praise, invisibly, but powerfully stir their consciousness - threaten the metaphysical foundations upon which they have erected the flimsy temples of their so-called well being - their systems - their plans - and what they perceive to be their "interests". So you will find (and this too was a revelation to me) that your "secret praise power" stirs up a certain degree of enmity - jealousy and malice towards you. This may scare you at first. Tempt you to make you stop. Obstruct your meditation. But the way out is MORE PRAISE. Increase it[8].

Isn't it wonderful that all of this is happening? Isn't it wonderful that they are jealous of you? Isn't it wonderful that they are attacking? Isn't it a fabulous revelation? Isn't it a fabulous insight into things?

Isn't it wonderful that their inner/secret attitudes are being flushed to the surface so that you can see their true character and recognize what you're dealing with? Isn't it fabulous that your inner work is working and that these "opposers" are coming out to meet you? Isn't it wonderful that your praise power is working and bringing your kingdom of heaven to pass?

Isn't it wonderful that the materialists can't understand you?

Isn't it fabulous that such and such a relationship broke up?

Isn't it rapture that you didn't get that job that you wanted?

Isn't it wonderful that things are working out the way they are?

In the beginning of such practices a part of you will undoubtedly feel that the "materialistic" position is correct. For, if the truth be told, we all have that aspect in our consciousness. You will feel - at first - that you're "lying" to yourself - deceiving yourself. You will feel tremendous opposition within yourself to the work that you're doing. You will need a strong will. I'm going to continue praising and that's that.

But if you persist, you will see how correct - metaphysically correct - your meditative procedure is. You will see precisely why things "REALLY ARE WONDERFUL". You will see how your attackers become powerless to harm you (they *never* had any power to harm you in the first place, except the power that you yourself gave them!). You will see your heart's desire manifest right in the middle of all the tumult/confusion/antagonism generated at you or towards you. You will understand clearly - by experience - the truth the psalmist uttered - "Thou preparest a table in the presence of mine enemies".

With Praise we are getting into a very scientific and workable principle of MIND which will eventually lead us into many other beautiful things. Praise your body and it immediately starts to improve - and sometimes material ways are revealed to even further improve it. Praise your home, your country, the people and things that you care about. Praise your enemies too - the most amazing things happen when you do this. Sometimes they cease to be "enemies" - the only thing that was creating the enmity was your psychic projection towards them. Sometimes you will see - and this sounds incredible! - that their enmity has blessed you in very profound and remarkable ways. In those cases you will actually secretly rejoice at their enmity. Praise your Divinity and you will see its operation and power in your life and affairs magnify and multiply. Praise your mind, the talents and abilities that you have. Praise your moods and sensations. Praise and magnify the Life Principle within you.

Watch what happens. Record it in your diary. Keep it secret.

It is wonderful!

10

The Ultimate Meditation

"There is a dimension in your soul where Wisdom speaks directly to the listening ear. It is a dimension of revelation open to all regardless of religion or ethnicity ... it is a place beyond religion – is in fact the source of that which is valid in all religions. In THAT place I Am ever with you and death does not exist."
The Magic Stone

Wisdom is the ultimate meditation. It is (along with the Will) the ultimate force on the mind level - and lest our *bhakti* brothers and sisters (and born again Christians) start getting riled and upset, let's explain.

The above statement is not meant in any way to belittle or demean the power of love or its importance. Indeed God is love, but he is also WISDOM. And there is NO CONTRADICTION between these two statements.

If love is the ultimate power on the *heart* or psychic plane - which it is - then wisdom is its counterpart on the level of mind.

Meditation on wisdom will not make a person less loving but to the contrary it will make them more loving - more effective lovers. Those who practice this will not love blindly but wisely. They will love benevolently.

What passes for love among some people is pretty ghastly - and there are situations where we would almost prefer their hatred and enmity than their so called love - what they perceive as love. In too many situations a lot of downright greed, ignorance, deceit and deception masks itself under the guise of love. All kinds of atrocities are committed in the name of love, which is why so many people are turned off to it. Love, to all too

66

many people (and even to those who presumable should know better), has become nothing more than a *button you push* in order to get some illegitimate advantage over another. To manipulate another against their lawful and legitimate interest. Disgusting really! What is needed is wisdom. Wisdom to illuminate our love - to widen it - to make it benevolent - to purify it - and to elevate it unto its rightful status.

Even thieves, robbers and petty con men have found it convenient to mask themselves in the guise of love - they have found it to be an effective coercive power on the psychological level which is perhaps a further tribute to the power of love - but those in contact with wisdom (which is an actual DIMENSION - an actual FORCE) will not be deceived. For they are in contact with the *real thing - the genuine article*. Like the experienced jeweler who is surrounded by real gold and gems for years and years, the wisdom being within each of us is not impressed by counterfeits.

Wisdom penetrates every facade. It sees motives. It recognizes only the *real*. It knows all about karma, past lives and all the ways to achievement. It knows the past and the future. It understands all the vagaries of the mortal plane but is not conditioned by it - but to the contrary the mortal plane MUST be conditioned by wisdom.

In the East the wisdom dimension is called *buddhi*. The Hebrews refer to it as *chochmah*. And when they call on the name of Jehovah it is this aspect that they call on. The Hebrews have called wisdom the "root of all greatness" - and indeed it is.

Wisdom (or the omniscience aspect of the divine) knows how to solve all your conundrums and paradoxes. For these things don't exist on that level. It knows what you need - it knows what you should do - it knows your place in the scheme of things and the answer to everyone of your questions. It knows all there is to know about money and health and success and all the things that you crave - and should have. And above all it is benevolent -

benevolence is its essence. Those who attempt to enter the wisdom spaces with malice in their hearts or from false motives find themselves repulsed and blocked - almost forced into a denial of that realm - and it is well that it should be so. For to them the dimension of wisdom doesn't exist - their own malicious thought processes block them from it.

When wisdom is *"let in or loosed"* in any mind that mind is instantly transformed to a certain degree. If the flow of wisdom is continuous - practiced regularly - the entire mind and consciousness will inevitably and inexorably be transformed. And not only will that particular mind be transformed but its vibrations - its omnipotent spiritual force – will transform other minds around the first - and even minds that are "apparently distant" from the meditator. It is wonderful Awesome. If you meditate you will see why and how this is to.

Wisdom has been called the great purifier. When let into the mind it will immediately - almost instantaneously expel all "obsessing entities" - first in the mind and intellectual processes, then in the heart and ultimately in the body. It will (given time) expel all malice, hatred, jealousy, fear, and other impurities of thought and feeling. It will increase the force and capacity of any mind it contacts. It will illuminate and reveal. It will show the true facts of any given situation on all the levels. It is the ultimate psychic defense.

It is especially good to call on wisdom when you feel confused. When you don't know what to do. When you feel ignorant about something or some situation or even some field of study. When you're not sure how so and so feels about such and such; or whether such and such a job is right for you; or when you feel really blocked in your meditation. It doesn't matter what it is - wisdom knows the way. Wisdom has the answer and is ready and willing to give it to you - if you allow it. For make no mistake about it, you have access to this dimension. It is your right and privilege to *go there* - to hold communion with it - to enter into it - and anyone who **willfully** blocks another from communion with wisdom - from entering this space - commits an act of aggression - an atrocity - on that soul. And such acts should be dealt with accordingly - in that light - as acts of aggression.

Please read Talbot Mundy's *I Say Sunrise* for a masterful description, discussion of the wisdom process. He was a gifted novelist (among the best in 20th century in my opinion) and describing the wisdom dimension taxed even his gigantic literary talent. Like all inspired writings the truth is between the lines. You must read it in a certain way - from a certain state of mind. Also very recommendable are the writings of Walter Lanyon. But you must meditate on them - go to the level of consciousness from which the work was written in order to truly understand it. This is the way to read all inspired writings - whether it be the Bible, the Vedas or Upanishads, the works of Aurobindo or Plato or whomever "does it for you." In this kind of writing the words and images are only guideposts to the thought - they are not meant to be taken too literally - but to sort of guide the mind to a desired space where their meaning - their inner meaning - becomes easily apparent. Cultural Pharisees and Philistines will find them *contradictory - imprecise - vague - nebulous - slippery - unscientific*, etc. and so it is for them. The meditator - the sincere heart - WILL penetrate and understand; will find no contradiction. It was designed that way.

A Meditation for Wisdom
Procedure
Center yourself between the eyes and declare yourself to yourself: "I Am An Immortal Spiritual Being At One with God and in Perfect Union and Harmony with the Universe."

Take a few deep, slow breaths. Visualize your aura of white light around you. Declare that nothing negative or malicious may enter you or emanate from you.

Bring your attention to the top of your head, and read the following out loud (this is more preferable, but if you can't do it out loud say it to yourself):

Divine Wisdom is flowing through my consciousness NOW!

OMMM OMMM OMMM (The chanting helps here!)

AHHH EHHH EEEE OOOO UUUU.

Divine Wisdom is flowing through every area and department of my life.

OMMM OMMM OMMM AHHH EHHH EEEE OOOO UUUU.

Divine Wisdom is flowing through every cell, organ, limb and physical feature of my body.

OMMM OMMM OMMM AHHH EHHH EEEE OOOO UUUU.

Divine Wisdom is flowing through my heart, my love life and social life.

OMMM OMMM OMMM AHHH EHHH EEEE OOOO UUUU.

Divine Wisdom is flowing through my financial life and consciousness.

OMMM OMMM OMMM AHHH EHHH EEEE OOOO UUUU.

Every time you make a statement repeat the chant. Feel the flow of the wisdom energy coming from over the head through your body.

If there is a situation confronting you that is crisis filled or confusing to you, think of the situation - hold it clearly in your mind - and say: "Divine Wisdom is flowing through this situation. Divine Wisdom is illuminating this matter."

Repeat this over and over again until you feel a sense of release. Sometimes this release happens instantly, sometimes it takes more time - but every time the situation comes to your mind repeat the affirmation that "Divine Wisdom is flowing through it." watch what happens. You will not only understand the situation with a newfound clarity but you will probably be in command of it. It will either dissolve or you will know exactly how to deal with it in the most effective, compassionate way.

If there is an organ or part of your body that is sick. Think of the organ or part and affirm that "Divine Wisdom is flowing through that organ or limb now" - repeat the statement until you feel a release - an answer. You will definitely get one. And it will always lead to improvement on the deepest possible levels.

Is there some subject at school that you find difficult? Before you begin to study, take a few moments and affirm that Divine Wisdom is illuminating me now - Divine Wisdom is illuminating my consciousness on this subject (name the subject) NOW." your studies will go much easier and better.

Things will start to improve for you in the most interesting ways - sometimes from within - sometimes through others.

Record your experiences in your diary.

It is glorious!

I I

The Yoga of Rapture

"Joy is the health of the soul."

"One cannot deny with impunity that which our being knows from all past experiences."

Fiery World

We are getting into a very controversial subject here and each of you will have to do your own clear thinking about it. But I will make this assertion - Rapture - the Spiritual Consciousness of Rapture - is available and accessible to each and every one of you. You are entitled to this rapture. In fact real spirituality is almost impossible without a steady, secure sense of Joy.

Those who are REALLY coming from "Thy Will Be Done" are a joyful people - though they may not be overly demonstrative about it. But if you are ever around one of these people you will feel a deep sense of elation - a peaceful joy - a profound bliss - seemingly without reason. For this bliss comes to them not from "outer circumstances" but as an "inner state" - from within. And this inner state is what we refer to when we talk about the Rapture.

People try all kinds of expedients to attain to this state - some use drugs, alcohol, sexual excess and every kind of "outer invention" imaginable - all for the purpose of feeling the rapture. And though they may touch it for a time through these expedients, the results are not lasting. For they have in a sense invaded - unlawfully - certain spaces to which they were not entitled to be according to the level of their consciousness. They are like "burglars". They cannot maintain this state normally - by right of their discipline, understanding and inner power - and so they touch it and fall back to the old spaces as soon as the stimulus of the "outer expedient" wears off - whether it be the drug or the alcohol or whatever. They have not dealt with the true causes of their pain and depression - not conquered the citadels of fear, ignorance, hatred - and so they enter the Kingdom of Heaven not as citizens of the realm - not as conquerors and overcomers - but as burglars - invaders and evaders. The least little nudge sends them back to their depression. They are not ESTABLISHED in the consciousness of the Bliss.

And yet the Rapture is available to them. Always there waiting for them. This is the paradox.

We need some clarity on the "Philosophical Level" here. Rapture means many things to many people. The average conception of Rapture is that of Sexual Bliss - people identify it with ONLY that. This is a big misconception and probably accounts for much of the general hostility towards the whole concept.

It is true that Sex is undeniably one of the Great Raptures on the physical plane - but the Rapture we refer to is MORE than that. We refer to a spiritual force. An aspect of God. Spiritual Rapture is "unconditioned and unconditional". It is not dependent on ANY material condition. And is the CAUSE - stands in a CAUSAL relationship - with all that the body considers to be pleasurable.

What we're saying here is that if one contacts (even for a brief instant - and a brief instant is better than nothing) the Spiritual Consciousness of Rapture (our Eastern Brothers call it Ananda) it will Cause "happy/rapturous/pleasurable" events on the physical plane.

Even thinking about the Rapture is a healthy exercise - even though we may not "feel" it right away. For the thought will lead to the feeling and then to the experience.

The Spiritual Consciousness of Rapture is the TRUE cure for grief, sorrow and depression. Everything else is just a temporary expedient - a band aid - a quick fix.

Rapture (the Spiritual State) will not only cure depression in oneself but in all those around the meditator - even strangers will feel the vibrations of the rapture.

The big difference between Rapture and what we commonly call pleasure is not only the "intensity" of the experience - pleasure is nowhere near as intense or vivifying as Rapture - but in the nature of the experience. Pleasure refers only to the sense world. We eat a good meal we feel pleasure. But Rapture happens on many levels at once. There is a mental and emotional ecstasy as well as the physical pleasure. In Rapture the physical sensations are actually the least important.

Rapture will cure depression in many ways. It lifts the soul up to another level of perception. Knowledge is revealed to the soul. Problems are solved on deep, deep levels. It is not only the "body" that feels good but the Mind and emotions as well. Rapture lifts one above the vibrations of the Earth.

Rapture is very different from "carousing" and irreverence. The Raptured one is very "reverend" - sometimes solemn - sometimes in a state of Awe - never disrespectful or malicious. He is "high" but he is totally clear minded. Alert. Perceptive.

As the consciousness gets adjusted to Rapture - and there is a big adjustment to make - it acquires more capacity to absorb and radiate it into the world. And this is a great Service. There are enough people - too many people - who are polluting the Divine Mind with pain, anguish and depression.

Hard to get established in Rapture - secure in it - until we deal with important theological and philosophical issues. One of them being, that the Nature of the Divinity IS rapturous. This is as much of what God is as any of the other attributes and principles that we attribute to THAT. Think about that. Mull it over. You will see that it is so. And the Saints/Adepts/Seers of almost every major religion - right across the board - testify to this fact.

God the All Perfect Omnipotence could have nothing to be "depressed about". Rapture would be its normal state.

If we transform/remove the pain, memories of pain, the weakness, hatred, malice, inadequacy, irritation and the other "impurities of thought" mentioned in Part 3 you will discover the rapture. Underneath all the surface emotions you will find a "stillness and a rapture".

When we make the God-Union (which happens to be a spiritual fact) consciously - when we affirm ourselves to be One with God - we are uniting with ALL of his attributes, including Rapture. So you can look forward to your moments of communion.

There are big adjustments to make. But it is worth it. One difficult adjustment is to learn to come from "rapture" in all our daily activities. We should work from rapture - go to the office in rapture - function from Rapture. But this will require some training.

There are those who affirm that "suffering is good for the soul" - and perhaps this is true at certain stages of ingrained materialism - there is no other way for these souls to grow. But God never ordained suffering - it was never divinely willed - couldn't have been willed - but is merely caused by a human's gift of free will (which *Was* ordained), a free will that was abused.

To those who say that suffering is good for the soul I say, Suffering might have its good points, but Rapture is infinitely better.

The only virtue that pain and suffering have is in the overcoming of them.

However, there is always free will, and those of you who prefer pain and depression may have it - I will not stop you. But personally, I'll take the Rapture.

A Meditation for Rapture

Center yourself between the eyes and say:

I Am an Immortal Spiritual Being, One with God and in Perfect Union and Harmony with the Universe.

I Am the Rapture of God.

I Am in a state of Rapture.

I Am the Rapture of All Good All Now.

Divine Rapture flows through me and from me to all points in my universe. Divine rapture fills my universe now.

Divine Rapture flows through my consciousness now.

I Am in Spiritual Rapture.

I Am in Mental and intellectual Rapture.

I Am in emotional/psychic Rapture.

I Am feeling Rapturous/Joyous feelings.

I Am experiencing Rapturous/joyous events, circumstances and conditions.

I Am doing rapturous/joyous things.

I Am in Social Rapture.

I Am in Financial Rapture.

I Am in Domestic Rapture and Harmony.

I Am in Rapturous Health.

I Am the Divine Rapture.

I look rapturous.

I think rapturously.

I feel rapturous.

I live and act rapturously.

Rapture is my normal and natural state.

So Mote it be. Amen.

If you like you can chant either the OM or the Vowels or EEE AHHH OHHH in between each statement. I have found this to be effective. But the statements have power in their own right.

12

Some Principles of Psychic Self-Defense

"Ye scoff at dreams? Thy world and everything in it was once a dream in the Creator's Mind. Ye think life begins at sunrise, but thine earthly life is naught but a dream of the sleeping spirit."
Master of Destiny

When one does the "Thy Will Be Done" ritual (as described in Part I) on a regular basis - and it should be done every day - the consciousness begins to transform. The meditator begins to live in the REAL world (as Vitvan calls it) - the world of energy and vibration. One begins to be sensitive to "frequencies" - to respond to them. One begins to discern the "good" and the "destructive" frequencies. A new sense is born - or opens up.

The meditator or "treader of the way" is never again the "slave of objective appearances". Little by little he/she discerns the reality - the vibration - beneath every image - every word. This is the most natural thing in the world.

He/she becomes conscious of the Psychic world - the world of thought-feeling - first. This becomes just as real - objective - as the physical world has been. And the psychic world - the Astral Plane as some call it - has "many mansions" - many kinds of energies. Some energies are incredibly beneficent, benevolent and healthy; others are abominably destructive.

The way Nature, in her Wisdom, has arranged things, one cannot progress to "higher levels" until one has "mastered" the psychic plane - subjected it to his/her will.

This mastery and dominion is your lawful and legitimate right. There's nothing to be ashamed of about it. We're supposed to do it. It was ordained. The Son of God - Man in his true nature

77

- IS MASTER of the psychic realms. It was created and designed that way. Mastery in this context does not mean being some kind of "astral bully" - abusing others or anything like that. It means being in control of your forces. In control of your own energy. Being able to accept a given vibration or keep it out. Being able to discern the vibration and deciding whether you want it in or out. This is very important, for as we mentioned some energies are ultra destructive - malicious - disruptive - inharmonious - unhealthy and we are no more meant to take that into ourselves than we are meant to eat poisonous food. It's that simple.

Being able to protect yourself psychically is one of the main challenges on the Path - and also in life. Not only can't you meditate effectively without developing this skill - but you can't live and function correctly either.

With the rituals given in Parts 4, 5 and 6 you have tools to "break" any negative state. But there are further things you should know.

A steady "attunement" or "connectedness" with your "highest Genius" - the Divinity whom you worship (under whatever name you worship it) is the first and most important line of defense. That Genius KNOWS clearly - with no possibility of error - exactly what's going on and exactly what to do about it. Learn to obey its "prompting and leading".

Avoid self-denial, self-diminishment of yourself and avoid doing it to others. Recognize the greatness in yourself and recognize it in others. God indwells there too though perhaps "deeply disguised".

Claim your right to the absolute "best" that you can envision for yourself at your "evolutionary state" and grant others the same right and privilege. By all means you are entitled to build your "personal Nirvana" on earth. To manifest your Personal Idea of The Kingdom of Heaven in your mind, body and affairs, but allow others the same right.

Keep your desires "constructive and beneficent" - and this is a lot easier to say than to do. For there is no action possible without doing "some sort of damage" to someone's interest somewhere. If I decide to eat bacon and eggs for breakfast - a seemingly innocuous choice - I have perhaps deprived "waffle manufacturers" of some income - aside from the fact that a pig - a living creature - was killed because of me. If I buy the New York Times in the morning, have I not injured the New York Post? If I buy a synthetic sweater have I not injured the Wool and Cotton industry? If I buy a wool sweater then I injure the synthetic industry. Being perfectly "harmless", as our Eastern Brothers advocate, seems totally impossible.

And yet they are correct. For though being perfectly harmless might be "impossible" we should strive for our good with the consciousness of doing the "least amount of harm" possible. Whether or not it is possible to be totally harmless - absolutely harmless - I will leave up to you. It's an important theme for meditation. Everyone will arrive at their own answer in their own way. But we can certainly look for ways to manifest our desires in the Least Harmful way possible. This is what I think our Eastern Brothers are driving at.

When confronted with a choice of two or three evils - a treader of the way will choose the lesser - the least damaging way.

When confronted with a need to obtain or do something the Treader of the Way will meditate - calculate inwardly - the way that does the most good and causes the least amount of damage.

There are times - sad to say - that destruction will be inevitable. The Treader of the Way will apply only enough "destruction" to "get the job done" and not an ounce more than necessary.

These are the "little signals" by which meditators now each other.

All of this sounds "very preachy" and if so, so be it. But important elements of psychic defense are contained here. Elements that the ancient Wise Ones understood very clearly and left with us. Living with these principles will minimize the amount of negativity that you arouse against yourself and your efforts.

Whatever freedom you claim for yourself give to others. Claim every right and privilege but grant it unto others. The Golden Rule operates on the metaphysical planes as well as on the physical.

Avoid meddling in other people's affairs as much as possible. If you are called in to help - specifically requested - then by all means do so. If you are not asked - stay out. There's enough of your own legitimate work to do without mixing into other people's business - even with good intentions.

The object of Meditation is NOT (as so many like to proclaim) "helping people". This is a shocking statement so I'm going to repeat it. The object of Meditation is NOT to help people. It is to reach a state of "union" with your Divinity. Paradoxically, when this is done correctly people DO get helped, therapized, healed, etc. But this is more of the nature of a "Side Effect" than a goal. This too should be taken into meditation. The people who are loudly proclaiming how much they've done and their need to "help" - are usually spiritual busybodies - meddlers - and in most cases are coming TOTALLY from their "personal sense of ego". For them it is another form of ego inflation. They either want something from you - want to take some unlawful/illegitimate advantage over you - want something for nothing - or want to start a "movement" of some kind. Be very careful. Discern the vibration. A word to the wise is sufficient.

When one renders help from a state of union with their divinity - from the Higher Spaces - it is always done with recognition of what the "other" really and truly needs - and always in their (the others) highest and best interest.

The bubble of white light referred to in Part 1 should be worked on diligently - strengthened as much as possible. Keep it around you not only when you open yourself in meditation but whenever you have to go into "hostile" situations or vibrations. Silence and secrecy about your work will also minimize (it won't completely eliminate) the antagonistic forces against you. Many people have trouble with silence because they fear its a "loss of intimacy" especially with loved ones. But I have found that with those who are truly on my "wavelength" there is no reduction of intimacy but on the contrary - the silence heightens the intimacy. It is respected by the other.

13

More on Psychic Self-Defense

"Aye power can cause pain. Aye its abuse can be deadly. But without Power the Good that ye crave cannot manifest. Ye attackers of Power, what would ye do if ye had it? Ye already abuse whatever little fire has been entrusted to ye."
The Magic Stone

The Rainbow Aura

A. The beauty of this technique is manifold. First off, you can combine it with your color meditation and achieve a two fold purpose - you get the healthful benefits/energies of the colors and you build a mighty spiritual shield of defense at the same time.

B. The bubble of white light we talked about in Part I is a good defense. Many writers mention it. It is a classic defense. But the rainbow aura is less mentioned. And, it seems to me, that it is a more powerful defense.

C. **Procedure**
1. Center yourself between the eyes and declare to yourself that you are an "Immortal Being of Light, one with God and in perfect union and harmony with the universe".
2. Review the color meditation of Part IV. Do the meditation but start with the White Diamond Light first and work your way down the spectrum; i.e. white -> gold -> violet -> indigo -> blue -> green -> yellow -> orange -> red.
3. Each time you take in a color put an egg of that color around

you. You should feel and see yourself in a radiant/blazing/ pulsing egg of each color. Inhale the color and on the exhalation see your egg glow even brighter - more radiant.

4. Build the shield in layers. That is, keep the egg of white diamond light as the most inner layer. The golden egg is the second most inner layer. The violet goes on top of that - etc. etc. etc. It is like wearing many layers off clothing - only this time you're building with Light and Power.

5. Make note of whatever obstructed you in the visualizing process and do some "Touch and Let Go" on it.

6. Practice the exercise until it becomes second nature to you - until you can put it around you in all circumstances and in all conditions. Then and only then could it be said that you "have it" - "own it".

Notes on the Rainbow Aura

A. The colors should be as pure and as brilliant as you can make them.

B. When confronted with situations where someone is "agressing you" see the shield between yourself and the aggressor.

C. Don't worry about the length of time that it takes to achieve proficiency in this exercise. Whatever time it takes is time well spent. If it takes one year or ten years doesn't matter. Each attempt will strengthen you. Each attempt will be beneficial over the short and the long term.

D. When you become proficient in this exercise you can extend your "Rainbow of Protection" around your children, your loved ones, your home and possessions. You start to become a VERY USEFUL BEING!

E. If you are familiar with **Kabballa** you can intone the Divine Names while putting the colors around you. It is VERY powerful.

F. The Divine Names even by themselves are very potent protection. With the colors the results are dramatic.

G. It also helps to keep the thought (and perhaps to affirm a few times a day) that you are a "Radiant Rainbow Being" - that you are "the Radiant Rainbow Aura". Thoughts and affirmations like these strengthen auric field/shield.

An ancient practice of psychic self defense was the "magical circle" or "ring pass not" of the ancient Magi. The operator draws a circle around him/herself physically and mentally - a flaming blazing circle - through which "no evil" (undesirable energy) may pass. Three circles are drawn. One horizontally around the operator; the second vertically, north to south; and the third vertically from east to west. If the operator wants to keep some person/entity or vibration "out" he draws the circle between himself and the person/entity or whatever. If he chooses to "let someone in" he draws the circle around himself and the person/entity or whatever. This is effective but I have found the Rainbow Aura to be more effective - for me anyway. The interested student could perhaps try a combination of these 2 methods and see what happens.

Many Metaphysicians advocate putting the Light of the Christ (or the Sun - the meaning is essentially the same) around themselves for protection. This is a healthy practice. But again, it seems to me that the rainbow aura - which includes the Golden Light of the Sun - is more powerful - more versatile.

The Middle Pillar Ritual as described by Regardie in "THE MIDDLE PILLAR" and other works[10] is a powerful tool of psychic defense. But like anything else it needs to be practiced until one becomes proficient with it. It seems to me that the benefit are worth it. The Middle Pillar is in itself an effective defense against most disruptive/undesirable vibrations and it leads one - by magical/mysterious and wonderful ways to other even more effective defenses. This is the beauty of all of these exercises. They are good in themselves and always lead one to "new good" - "new vistas of good".

Of course, very little can protect one if he or she is in violation of some "Cosmic Law" or Principle - if one is coming from a position of "Untruth". In those situations there is little recourse but to get "back into alignment" as quickly as possible. But if you are in a correct position - a position of right and truth - all of the above are very effective defenses.

It is absurd to think that one can indulge in all kinds of malice/dishonesty/deceit and be "protected" - such protection - even the best - will be flimsy indeed.

The visualization of Archetypal Forms can also be used as powerful defenses. The Five Pointed Star; the Kabbalistic (equal armed) Cross; the Pyramid; the Cube; the Dodecahedron[11] (though this is a bit difficult to visualize) are all very effective. One can visualize oneself in a dazzling Pyramid of Light and keep it there before entering potentially "hostile" spaces. Any of the above-mentioned forms can be visualized around oneself as a shield. Personal experimentation is in order.

Olive Pixley in "THE ARMOR OF LIGHT" (in 2 parts) describes techniques that many (among them those I have high regard for) testify to be effective. But again these things need to be practiced. It's not something that happens overnight.

Dion Fortune's "PSYCHIC SELF DEFENSE" should also be studied.

There is a whole science-art of Talismanic Magic - a noble science - very lofty - which deals with the art of "charging inanimate objects" with any desirable frequency/vibration that one chooses. These are then used for healing or protection or whatever. This is beyond the scope of this series, but its well worth looking into on your own. As long as you realize that is not so much the "physical object" itself that does the trick but the"meaning/thought/will energy" that one "invests" or charges the object with that makes the magic - you'll be on safe ground. Otherwise we got lost in a welter of superstition and are probably worse off than before.

14

More Ways to Impress the Deeper Mind

"Come with me, like a priest of the Orphic mysteries, I will lead you into darkness of night through deep, moonless forests, the paths of the nether world leading to the gates of Hades. Do not be afraid; I have a torch and I know my way. You will not get lost. And at dawn, we will come to the temple of the rising sun."
The Red Lion

The Writing Out Technique

Please refer to Part II. In that part we described a ritual for "outing" undesirable/negative/destructive thoughts and feelings. We did this by "writing them out" ritualistically and with "conscious intent" to "out them".

Now we are going to use the same technique to impress the deeper mind (or subconscious if you prefer) with our own conscious and willed images/thoughts/desires. And by the Law of its Nature - the Law of its Being - we can expect it to come to pass in due course.

We are "reversing" the ritual - turning it inside out. Using it to "invoke" (bring in) rather than to banish (get rid).

Think of some desirable state, image or desire. It doesn't matter what it is. Do you want to lose weight? Do you need some money? Do you want a house? Health? Get specific. Get a clear image of what you want. Then center yourself between the eyes and remind yourself of who you are:

"I AM AN IMMORTAL BEING OF LIGHT - AN IMMORTAL SPIRITUAL BEING - ONE WITH GOD AND IN PERFECT UNION AND HARMONY WITH THE UNIVERSE."

Take a notebook - your Magical Diary is excellent for this purpose - and on a blank page write the following:

"I (write your name) am now consciously/clearly and perfectly visualizing, seeing, feeling, sensing, experiencing the following:"

Now write out your desire about 25 times. (Most notebooks have about 25 or so lines so you can measure yourself by using one full page.)

Let's say that your goal is to lose weight. Write out (and visualize to yourself as you write) "I am losing weight"; "I am getting slender and trim"; "My body is becoming as I desire it to be"; etc. Write this out 25 times and then let go.

Record your inner reactions in your magical diary. These are important. If they keep troubling you, you will have to do some touch and let go on them.

Repeat the writing out ritual daily (at some convenient time) until you start to get some "action/response" from your deeper mind. This starts happening anywhere from 2 weeks to 2 months depending on the nature of the desire.

Every time you "write out" you are in a sense "creating in Mother Substance" - the substance of "feeling". It is a very direct and powerful way to impress the Deeper Mind. It is especially useful for those who have "visualizing problems" for whatever reason. Also the fact that writing is a "physical motion" as well as an "intellectual action" brings the "lower centers" into operation. More centers are involved in the visualization process and the results become stronger.

If you are familiar with Kabballa you can preface the Writing Ritual with an intonation of the Divine Name/Sephira/Planetary Principle that "rules" the image or desire that you're working on.

If you are familiar with Astrology (and this is well worth getting into) you can time your Writing Ritual for periods when the planetary (celestial) influence are most favorable. It really makes a difference. When the influences are favorable the visualizing is stronger and the results are quicker. But this is something that you have to experiment with in order to prove. Right now you have to take my word for it.

I have had the most incredible experiences with the Writing Ritual. Dramatic releases. Inner "explosions". And of course, demonstration in very normal and natural and HONEST ways.

I have also seen - by the nature of my inner reaction to the image - exactly what was "obstructing" the manifestation. It is also wise (and very interesting!) to note the reactions of others towards you as you continue your daily writing practice. You will see the confirmation of the efficacy of your work in their "eyes and attitudes". It is a good way to learn who your real friends and enemies are. Your true friends will subconsciously support your work, help bring it to pass. The others will probably resent it - attack you for no apparent reason - they themselves might not be aware of the reason, but their resistance will "flare up".

It's worth mentioning that its a good idea to preface the ritual with the thought that you want manifestation "Under Grace in blessed and harmonious ways". Write this out after you've stated your intention.

I think it's also worth mentioning our definition of a "Good Demonstration or Manifestation". First off, it is honest. Secondly it is "good for all concerned" - for all who help bring it to pass. Third, it is harmonious. Fourth, it is practically effortless and stress free - there is no "coercion" involved. With a good demonstration/manifestation there is no deceit or manipulation involved. Everything is on the "up and up". Those who are supposed to "bring it to pass" WANT to bring it to pass.

When we use words like "effortless" - which are very controversial - we need to explain what we mean. Effortless doesn't mean that you "make no physical motions". Sometimes you do and sometimes you don't. Effortless means that whatever motions (physical motions) that you are called on to make will be effective, to the point and powerful. There will be relatively little "waste of energy". Everyone and everything cooperates during a good demonstration - a demonstration that has manifested naturally (not "hyped up", forced or coerced), honestly and under grace.

The Taping Technique

Again we are taking a previous exercise and "turning it inside out". This works very well with the Writing Out Ritual.

Take the desire that you've been writing about and "speak it into a tape". Sixty second continuous loop tape (the kind they use in answering machines) is very good to use. The tape will keep repeating itself over and over again - which is precisely what we want. Put the tape on when you go to sleep and go to sleep with it. Let it play - monotonously and repetitively - throughout the night. Let it lull you to sleep. Your deeper mind which "neither slumbers nor sleeps" will be deeply impressed by the message. Do this every night for a month or until your desire is manifest. Though there are many commercial tapes on the market for almost every conceivable need and/or desire - and many of them are pretty good - it seems to me that "your own voice" giving the message is still the best way.

Changes will start to occur in your life as they should - easily, effortlessly and relatively stress free.

Casting the Burden

Again, we are taking a previous exercise and "turning it inside out".

Think of your desire or need. Say to yourself firmly:

"I NOW CAST THE BURDEN OF THIS DESIRE (NAME THE DESIRE) UPON THE GOD WITHIN (UNDER WHATEVER NAME YOU ARE CALLING IT) AND I GO FREE IN HARMONY AND FULFILLMENT."

Repeat this over and over until you feel a "release" then stop.

One of two things will happen - and this is very interesting. You will either get the "thing" or desire" or you will stop feeling a "need or craving" for it. If the desire is something positive - something that you should have, you will certainly get it. If it is only something that you THINK that you want - something that will not really make you happy - you will lose the "craving" for it. It will cease to trouble you.

Try it. Record your results in your diary. Be silent and secret. You are on a "Great Adventure". And you are going to start meeting hosts of other souls who are also on the same adventure. You will know and recognize each other. Isn't it wonderful?

Touch and Let Go

This exercise can also be "reversed" and done on the "positive". The technique is basically the same as described in Part III. Just write your desire (in pencil) on a sheet of paper and touch it and let go. Whatever blockages exist to your desire will surface and discharge. You can also use a photograph of your desire.

Every time you touch the paper you are in a very real sense "calling up the image" of that desire - automatically and spontaneously. Also your personal reactions to the image. If you're reactions are negative you might want to do some touch and let go on the negative reactions - especially if there is some specific "fear image" or "painful memory" associated with the fulfillment of the desire in question.

Doing "touch and let go" on the positive and desirable is a wonderful way to break any "negative state". Negative states are usually caused by excess focus on the "painful and undesirable". Now you are putting the mind - in a very physical way - on to the positive and desirable. Please don't take my word for it. Try it.

15

Stress

"The essence of True philosophy is ease."
Talbot Mundy

It seems that everyone deals with this subject in one way or another and so we might as well add our own input.

It is widely recognized (even by the medical profession - and it's about time) that it is not disease that kills but STRESS. Stress causes disease. Stress creates the basic chemical imbalances that weaken and eventually damage the organism. So the big challenge, for those who are interested in their health, is how to avoid, minimize or eliminate stress.

There is no question that stress begins in the mind/emotions - in the psychic nature. And there are 2 major reasons for it. One major cause of stress - perhaps THE major cause - is being out of harmony or out of sync with the "Higher Will" - the Will of one's Higher Genius. Keep in mind that the Higher Will (the Will of the God Within) is the actual origin of all your thoughts and desires - your real thoughts and desires. It is also the Origin of the Life Force or Life Principle within a person. To be out of tune with this is to experience a "reduction of life force" and this is the first "unease" - the Primal Unease - Original Sin as some have called it. When there is a reduction of "life force" all the faculties are "diminished" - the power to think, to love, to resist disease, to sense, feel and perceive. This is a very dangerous condition to be in. If you think about it you'll easily see why.

The second major cause is being out of harmony with our fellow human beings - relationship problems. Even if one has - through logic methods or through any of the plethora of autosuggestive methods (many of which are quite good and we don't mean to imply any criticism here) achieved a relative state of physical relaxation - it is difficult to hold the state - to maintain it for any length of time. Thoughts arise in the consciousness - angry/hostile/resentful thoughts. Grievances, complaints, attack and counterattacking thoughts, pain and memories of pain arise in the consciousness - disturbing the tranquility that we are striving to achieve. These thoughts are like "angry wiggling fish in the water of our consciousness". Ripples and actual vortexes are created - first mentally - then in the physical body.

The first cause is easily cured - with time. We cure it by getting back in alignment with our Highest Genius and Letting its will be done in our mind, body and affairs without obstruction from us. This has been described in Part I. When you are One with Your Genius - when you are REALLY doing its will - you might very well become physically active - busier than you have ever been before - but there will be no stress in those kind of "actions". Very difficult to describe. The actions are powerful - effective - to the point - and ultra successful. Very little waste of time, energy, motion. Very little meandering or worry. Mighty works of power are done "in seconds" that by mortal standards should have taken years. Such actions are not only stress free but actually enjoyable - fun - rapturous. There is no sense of "laboriousness or inelegance" in such actions. For they are "natural" - part of the "general cosmic movements" - as much a movement of nature as a speeding planet on its predestined path. If you are REALLY coming from "Thy Will Be Done" you will Love everything that you are called on to do. And thus one of the major causes of stress (that of hating and despising what we do - despising our work) will be relieved.

The second major cause of stress - that of being out of harmony with our fellow humans - is probably "incurable" at this stage of the evolutionary process - though all of us look forward to the day when peace and harmony WILL reign on earth as it does in heaven. And though it seems "incurable" (at this time) it doesn't mean that we can't "relieve or reduce" the problem. We can. And we have discussed various ways of "reducing" the disharmony - "touch and let go" - Casting the Burden - minimizing the amount of hatred/malice/fear that we put out into the environment - psychic self-defense against the hostile projections of others - attitudes of tolerance and freedom - silence and secrecy etc. All of these will reduce the amount of stress that you are called on to bear without limiting your effectiveness - to the contrary you will be more effective in more ways than you ever dreamed possible.

The chanting of Om for prolonged periods tends to bring our mind and body back into a state of harmony and thus there is a reduction of stress. A normal and natural "lightness and euphoria" comes in.

If you have been practicing the techniques described in the previous parts - getting yourself "physically relaxed" will be very easy. For you will be more mentally and emotionally relaxed and thus the "last step" - that of relaxing the physical becomes normal and natural and easy. Almost any technique will work. You can "if you like" simply lie down and "command" the physical to happen. You can "Cast the Burden of Tension from anywhere in the Body upon your Inner Lord and `go free' in peace, harmony and relaxation". You can, while lying down, "auto-suggest" relaxation either by word or by image or both - repeat to yourself over and over again that you are "steadily getting more and more relaxed; that your muscles and organs are loosening and letting go" etc. etc. etc. You can hold the image of "a cat in repose"[12] as you suggest the relaxation to your deeper mind. You can hold the image while you listen to soft, soothing, harmonious music - there are many such tapes on the market.

Israel Regardie in "THE ART OF TRUE HEALING" has some interesting kabballistic methods for relaxation. Very Powerful. Very effective - but requires some practice.

Annie Payson Call in "POWER THROUGH REPOSE" and "THE FREEDOM OF LIFE" also goes deeply into this subject.

The International Sophrology Institute[13] has some very effective tapes for relaxation. They also offer courses and seminars to learn basic techniques for reducing stress.

Some imagery that some people find helpful for relaxation - choose the one that works best for you:

a. You are floating on a cloud on a clear sunny day.
b. Imagine yourself to be very tiny. You are floating on a leaf in a clear mountain lake. Some like to visualize themselves floating on a lotus blossom.

But if you want to get the most out of all of these effective methods you must clear yourself of "mental/psychic stress" and this is done by the ways that we have indicated previously.

It is possible to feel alert and totally relaxed while in the middle of a "combat zone" - to feel a sense of peace, safety and protection right in the center of all the chaos that surrounds you - to feel the "connection" and "guidance" from "above" under all conditions. For, like all the other Divine Ideas/Attributes that we've discussed - these are "inner states" - unconditional and unconditioned by the material world. On the contrary, the material world is in itself conditioned by these "Inner States". Experts can achieve this. So can you.

16

Three Approaches to Meditation

Like most people, after reading the reams of literature on the subject of meditation and "mind treatment", I was confused. This confusion lasted a long time. There were so many schools of thought, so many conflicting philosophies, so many systems, so many exercises, so many teachers, so many gurus - each apparently contradicting the other.

There was no way out of the maze except through experimentation with all of them - and this is not something one does in a year or so - or even ten years - or even ten lifetimes. To say the least, it is incredibly time consuming. Still we must begin where we are. I spent quite a while (by my personal standards) exploring these things and still there was confusion, until one day I happened to glance at the writings of the Hindu Saint Swami Yogananda.

I had been familiar with his work previously. Had in fact read the book in question many years before and was not especially impressed. But this time a passage fairly leaped out of the page and hit me in the face. I saw the truth that linked and unified all the different systems. It was like looking at it for the first time.

"Nothing happens before its Time" say the Adepts, and this was certainly so for me.

In just one paragraph he (very elegantly) cleared up the whole quagmire of argument, confusion and even animosity between various systems. He said that there were three ways to meditate - three ways to use the mind - three ways to work "mentally". One was the way of the Subconscious, the second was the way of the Conscious Mind and the third was the way of Super-consciousness. In order to be really effective one had to engage -

incorporate - ALL THREE aspects of the Mind (for these 3 minds are really ONE MIND.)

If we engage only one aspect of the Mind our work will have very little effect, for the bulk of the mind is not in harmony. If we get 2 out of the three aspects of mind to agree then our work will have some power - and we will probably demonstrate. But if we get all 3 minds to cooperate - to agree with what we're doing - we start to perform Miracles. The power starts to become awesome.

Based on this perception we can now start to catalogue all the different systems that we come across. We can put them into perspective and understand where they fit in.

All the systems that deal with "visualizing" - forming mental images - repeating affirmations over and over again - chanting some phrase or sound over and over again - are all dealing with the *Subconscious Aspect of Mind*. What some call the "Lower Self". This mind is the "habit mind" and its job is to execute all commands and ideas that penetrate it.

This kind of working is called "moon magic" or the "lesser magic". For it deals with our personal selves - our personal feelings - our personal environment. It deals with our Microcosm. It is impressed by "images" and constant repetition. It is also very much impressed by Ritual - actions that are repetitive.

Systems that emphasize "setting goals" - planning - reasoning - organization - right thought - right concepts - right words - clear thinking - clear logic - right attention - concentration - are all dealing with the *Conscious Aspect of Mind*. These systems are called "Hermetic Magic" or Hermetics.

Systems that emphasize "contact with Divinity" - the Higher Self - invocation - prayer - supplication - entreaty - devotion - are all dealing with the *Superconscious Aspect of Mind*. This is called the "Greater Magic" - the Magic of Light.

The Conscious Mind directs thought and energy and makes all decisions. The Subconscious carries out orders. The Super

Conscious Illuminates and inspires.

Some systems emphasize one approach over another and thus they are inadequate. For example, many psychologists (not all of them) know the Laws of the Subconscious but they behave as if Super Consciousness did not exist! So, all of their mental work is based strictly on "human standards" of evaluation. Others, behave as if the Subconscious didn't exist - as if only their will and reason existed. Others - especially the Religious Types focus only on Superconsciousness - the Realm of the Divine - and make that paramount - often ignoring the other aspects of mind.

What is needed for effective work is the use of all 3 minds.

A method that works with Subconsciousness will be ineffective with Superconsciousness. Superconsciousness (the Dimension of Wisdom, Understanding - the Space from where the Original Will emanates) is not at all impressed with our rituals or repetitions. The fact is that WE (as humans) cannot impress it at all. We can only invoke - turn our attention to it and say - in effect - Thy Will Be Done. We are impressed by IT and not vice versa.

The invocatory techniques for Superconsciousness are inappropriate for Subconsciousness - for there WE are the BOSS. WE tell it what to do. WE impress it.

The proper way to work is to first get the Light and Inspiration from Superconsciousness - God - and from that space of Light and Understanding learn to observe and reason correctly (the Conscious Mind) and then impress the subconscious mind with correct ideas, concepts and directions.

Sometimes we access Superconsciousness by means of the subconscious and sometimes we access the subconscious by means of the Superconscious. This is a matter of personal preference.

If you reread the previous parts of this series you will see that we used techniques that engage all the minds.

When you preface an exercise or ritual with the statement:

"In the Name of the Wisdom, the Love, the Justice and the Mercy of the One Eternal Spirit" (Or some other similar formula)

you are, in effect, "involving" the light and power of Super-Consciousness.

When you organize your goals on your Treasure Map, putting down possible means and methods of attainment you are using your conscious mind.

When you do the chanting or breathing exercises you are working with the Subconscious Mind by means of the Conscious Mind.

When you use the Command Phrase Technique - or Touch and Let Go - you are working on BOTH the Conscious and subconscious mind.

The Meditation for Wisdom (Part X) will expand the conscious mind and indirectly the subconscious mind.

All of this is important to understand. For you now have three ways to deal with any problem - a conscious way (Reason, Will, Order, Organization, Study, Planning etc.) - a subconscious way (Creating desirable mental images, installing desirable concepts, either by ritual or by constant repetition) - and a Superconscious way (Invoking Wisdom, Invoking your own highest concept of God and letting its Will and Light come in - prayer and devotion.)

Footnotes

[1] This was written in the 1980's, now I understand that you can get these books online.

[2] Though I used the OM to illustrate how to work you don't need to use it - some people have "mental blocks" with OM - for various reasons. You can use I.A.O. or the Vowels and get equally good results. Some people get results from just repeating the affirmation without using any form of chant - I've had many experiences like that - but there's no question that the chant adds power to the affirmation and builds up a stronger "mental image" of the desired "thing".

[3] Ophiel, *the Art and Practice of Getting Material Things Through Creative Visualization*, Weiser, 1967.

[4] *The Art and Practice of Getting Material Things Through Creative Visualization*. WEISER. 1967.

[5] *The Miracle of New Avatar Power*, Parker Publishers. This is an excellent piece of work - deceptively simple - written in plain language. However we recommend a lot of work on Part 2 and Part 3 of Technique for Meditation before using it. It is pure Kaballa to which he has attached different labels.

[6] Ibid

[7] About the kindest thing - the most praiseworthy characteristic - that we can find to say about our blessed materialists is that they DO in fact crave, yearn for, and seek REALITY. The kindest definition I have heard about Materialism was given by a Master in a work called "FIERY WORLD" - and he said that Materialism was

the soul's search for reality at a certain stage of evolution. And for this we praise them. For if this is indeed their motive their search will ultimately lead them to knowledge of the Higher Worlds - some sooner, some later.

[8] Please see THE CRAFT OF METAPHYSICS by this author for some ways of proceeding. Also the writings of Walter Lanyon - if meditated upon - yield a lot of light on this issue.

[9] Vitvan was a 20th century American Master. He founded a school called the School of the Natural Order in Baker, Nevada. His writings - and they are numerous - are available direct from the school. They are highly recommendable though one needs considerable intellectual background to penetrate them.

[10] Also see *"The Art of True Healing"* by Israel Regardie, where he goes into a very detailed explanation of the exercise.

[11] The Dodecahedron is a 12 sided solid - each side equal - and is the archetypal form of the universe.

[12] Dr. Rolf Alexander in *"the Power of the Subconscious Mind"* suggests this method. He also suggests visualizing the muscles as "loose strands of wool" for achieving relaxation.

[13] This organization no longer exists, but their materials could be available on line.

BOOKS

O is a symbol of the world, of oneness and unity. In different cultures it also means the "eye," symbolizing knowledge and insight. We aim to publish books that are accessible, constructive and that challenge accepted opinion, both that of academia and the "moral majority."

Our books are available in all good English language bookstores worldwide. If you don't see the book on the shelves ask the bookstore to order it for you, quoting the ISBN number and title. Alternatively you can order online (all major online retail sites carry our titles) or contact the distributor in the relevant country, listed on the copyright page.

See our website www.o-books.net for a full list of over 500 titles, growing by 100 a year.

And tune in to myspiritradio.com for our book review radio show, hosted by June-Elleni Laine, where you can listen to the authors discussing their books.

9781846944123